BRING the
BACK Joy

WOMEN OF FAITH [SM]

Bring Back the Joy is based on the popular
Women of Faith conferences.

Women of Faith is partnering with Zondervan
Publishing House, Integrity Music, *Today's Christian Woman*
magazine, and Campus Crusade to offer conferences,
publications, worship music, and inspirational gifts that
support and encourage today's Christian women.

Since their beginning in January of 1996, the Women of Faith
conferences have enjoyed an enthusiastic welcome by women
across the country. Women of Faith conference plans presently
extend through the year 2000. Call 1-888-49-FAITH
for the many conference locations and dates available.

www.women-of-faith.com

WOMEN OF FAITH℠

BRING BACK the Joy

*Rekindling
the Joy in Your
Relationship
with God*

SHEILA WALSH

WITH EVELYN BENCE

ZondervanPublishingHouse
Grand Rapids, Michigan

A Division of HarperCollinsPublishers

*This book is dedicated
to all Women of Faith*

Also by Sheila Walsh

Honestly
Gifts for Your Soul

Other Women of Faith Books for You to Enjoy

Joy Breaks
The Joyful Journey, book and audio
Friends Through Thick and Thin
We Brake for Joy!, book and audio (available July 1998)

CONTENTS

ACKNOWLEDGMENTS

Sheila wishes to thank the following people:

Ann Spangler, for her assistance in editing this project.

Evelyn Bence. It was a joy to work with you on this one, Evelyn. Our time was limited, but you offered your companionship every step of the way. When I was tired you gave yourself to put fresh wind in my sails. Thank you so much.

My fellow Women of Faith, whose friendship continues to bring joy to my life.

Steve Arterburn, whose vision began this Joyful Journey and whose friendship deepens along the way.

My darling husband, Barry, and little lamb, Christian, who make me laugh till tears run down my cheeks and daily remind me of the faithfulness of God.

Evelyn extends her thanks to Camilla Luckey for inspiration at just the right moment.

PART 1

ENVISIONING THE JOY

Joy is the serious business of heaven.
C. S. Lewis

R ed rover, red rover, let Sheila come over."
They chose me! Only a silly school game. But they chose me! I ran with every ounce of energy I had, the cold Scottish wind pressing against my face as if in league with the other team. As I ran I identified the weak link in the human chain ahead of me, and I threw myself against it, willing it to give. At first the line seemed to hold, but I pressed on and the two girls parted, letting me run through, scoring a point for my team.

Moments of joy from childhood.

Lying on the grass, face to the sky, hands caressing the soft green velvet at my fingertips. No more school for eight glorious weeks. Visions of picnics on the beach and day trips to Glasgow and Edinburgh and the school-days' bedtime lifted for the summer ... bliss.

Early Christmas morning! Waking up in a cold bedroom, frost on the windowpanes, snow draping the trees outside my window. Wrapping up in warm dressing gowns and slippers, my brother, Stephen, my sister, Frances, and I woke my mother and my grandmother at some unearthly hour to see if "he" had been there yet. Creeping down the stairs barely able to contain the excitement. Opening the living room door ... a wonderland, a transformation overnight from the ordinary to every unspoken wish laid out in gold and red and green packages. Tangerines wrapped in silver paper. The aroma of turkey filling every room. "Hark, the herald angels sing...."

Simple joy. Pure wonder. Hopes and dreams. Anything is possible. I see it again as a forty-one-year-old mother of a baby boy. Our first autumn. We sit out on the deck surrounded by spent leaves. He gathers them in his arms and laughs as they crumble in his tiny hands. We play peekaboo for what seems like hours and he laughs and laughs. His grandfather walks into the room, and baby Christian's face lights up as if he knows the show is about to start. My son finds a leftover Cheerio on the carpet and examines it, turning it over and over, fascinated by this simple gift. I see things I haven't noticed in years through his eyes and I wonder why our vision becomes impaired with the turning of calendar pages. Perhaps we have forgotten what joy looks like.

CHAPTER 1

INDESCRIBABLE DELIGHT

Though you have not seen him, you love him; and even though you do not see him now, you believe in him and are filled with an inexpressible and glorious joy.

1 Peter 1:8

When I met Christ, I felt that I had swallowed sunshine.

E. Stanley Jones

I wonder what pictures come to your mind when you think of joy? I think of moments from my childhood. I think of picnics in Belisle Country park in my hometown of Ayr, Scotland, with my mom and Frances and Stephen. We would play in the sun for hours and then gather on a plaid blanket to feast on tomato sandwiches—my favorite.

I remember an old tree in the park that looked like a horse, and we rode for miles on that trusty steed.

I think of long walks on Sunday afternoons. I loved to walk by the river Ayr up to the stepping stones. We would stand in the middle of the river and skip pebbles across the surface of the water.

As I look back on my childhood now, I know that we didn't have much money. My mother has never owned her own house or driven a car, but we were rich in moments of simple joy. We loved each other. We talked to each other and we listened. We rode bikes together and played board games and listened to music. We read books and we sang around our old piano. Simple life. Simple joy.

I wonder what memories come to you? Perhaps we share similar precious moments. But maybe you are reluctant to turn your mind to days that were filled with pain, and you feel cheated of what should have been days of innocence.

BRING BACK THE JOY

I remember the day when Andy Hendron, the boy who lived across the street, told me that there was no Santa Claus. I was devastated. I ran into the house, past my mother, up the stairs to my room where I threw myself on my bed and sobbed. I heard a gentle knock on the door. It was my mom. "Is it true?" I asked her through my tears. My mom explained to me that Santa Claus was a fun game we had played, but that the real meaning of Christmas—the real gift of the Christ child—was true. "But now I won't get any gifts!" I cried.

"Of course you will," my mother assured me. And all was well.

But we grow up and myths are dispelled, hearts are broken, promises not kept. We move into the real world and leave joy behind on the nursery floor like an old discarded toy or a childhood Sunday school chorus: "I've got the joy, joy, joy, joy, down in my heart."

Perhaps that's why we love to have children around at Christmas. For a few moments we can forget the worries of unpaid bills, the illnesses of loved ones, or a troubled marriage, and we can recapture a little of the uncluttered wonder of life reflected in big blue eyes. But then it's over for another year, and, for some, Christmas is the most painful time of all.

So can joy be found again?

Can joy be discovered if we've hardly tasted it at all?

Yes. And that's my story.

In 1997 I was invited to be part of a team of six Women of Faith speakers who traveled under the name "The Joyful Journey." I knew Barbara Johnson, having interviewed her when I was cohost of *The 700 Club* on the Christian Broadcasting Network. I knew of Luci Swindoll and Patsy Clairmont, although we'd never met. Marilyn Meberg and Thelma Wells were new faces and names. When Barry, my husband, Christian, our son, and I flew to Hawaii for the first conference, I had no idea that the chance to work with these women and be with them would be the best Christmas gift ever.

I grew up in a small town on the west coast of Scotland. When I was four my father died of complications from a brain hemorrhage. Before he died his personality changed drastically. I didn't understand why. Had I done something wrong? Did he see something in me that made him change how he felt about his beloved tomboy daughter? I made a silent commitment never to let anyone down again. I would be the perfect good-girl.

When I was eleven I went with family and friends to hear the Heralds, a Scottish gospel group. I listened on the edge of my seat as Ian Leitch, the evangelist, spoke. "God has no grandchildren, only sons and daughters," he said. That evening I got down on my knees with my mom beside my bed and asked Jesus to take control of my life. In my head I knew it was a gift to be loved by God, but in my soul I determined to work to be worthy of the gift so that it would never be taken away. "If a daddy can stop loving," I reasoned, "I guess God can too."

At nineteen I went to Bible College in London. When I graduated I joined Youth For Christ on a missions team to Europe. Then I came to America and made it my home. I traveled all over the country as a singer and speaker and was spotted during an interview on television by Jackie Mitchum, the guest coordinator for *The 700 Club*. Pat Robertson had recently returned to the show from his run for president and was looking for a new cohost. I was invited to fly in and interview and was given the job that first day. For almost five years I interviewed everyone from Billy Graham to Smokey Robinson, from Hulda Buntain (a gentle missionary to India) to Charlie Daniels.

I loved my job, but my life was catching up with me. I had carried such a load of self-doubt and shame for so many years, I was exhausted. I had kept all my rules that I thought made up the perfect Christian, but I wasn't sure it would ever be enough. In the fall of 1992 my world came crashing in on me, and I was hospitalized for severe clinical depression. Everything I was afraid of had happened. I didn't want to let anyone down, and now I was letting twenty million viewers down badly. I was buried under the grief and shame of it all.

And then a miracle happened. I went one Sunday to a small church in Washington, D.C., just a few miles from the hospital. It was as if God had given the pastor a letter to read from God's heart to mine. The pastor said, "Some of you feel as if you're dead inside, as if you can hear them begin to pile the earth on top of your coffin. Christ is here. If you will ask him to, he will reach down and pull you from this pit and put your feet on solid ground."

It was as if I'd never heard it before. I ran to the front of that church and threw myself before the altar. I came empty-handed. That was a first for me. I had always brought a little something that I thought would make God happy, whether it was a new book or a record or letters from viewers saying that they had been helped by something I said. Not this time. I came with nothing.

There is a song that goes,

Nothing in my hand I bring
Simply to thy cross I cling.

I finally got it! I finally understood that God loves me because that is who he is. There is nothing I can do to make it happen. It already has. I find it hard to put into words the joy that began in the darkest place inside of me and finally fell out of my lips in laughter. All the efforts I had made to make myself lovable had been pointless and frustrating. Without God, without what Jesus has already done for me, I'm not lovable at all, but because of him I am loved with a love that will last forever. It's a gift, not a deal. Pure gift! For most of my life I kept people at a distance, afraid of what they would see if they got too close; I was very public on the outside but deeply lonely inside. Now I could be myself, confident in the eternal love of God. It was like taking off support hose and breathing deeply for the first time!

That's where I'd been. Then, early in 1997, at my first Joyful Journey conference, there I was, sitting on stage with five relative strangers. I had no idea what to expect. God had a big surprise in store for me. As each woman took the stage, I heard a familiar tune in her words. It was being sung in five different ways, but it was the same song, and I knew it too. It said, "Life is tough, but God is faithful." It said, "You can know real joy in the midst of the pain of life." It said, "Celebrate your moments. Life is now!"

I looked out at the faces of the women who sat in the arena and watched as they drank in each word. Joy in the midst of life. Joy in the presence of pain. Joy as we were always meant to know it. Does that seem like wishful thinking to you?

As you sit and read these words, do you feel you're being pressured one more time to pull yourself together and be a joyful Christian woman? Then think again. Because joy is a gift that you didn't order, can't pay for, and don't deserve.

As I have discovered joy, I can see how it reconnects us to the indescribable delight and wonder of childhood. As Jesus said, "I tell you the truth, unless you change and become like little children, you will never enter the kingdom of heaven" (Matthew 18:3).

At age fifty-one Madeleine L'Engle wrote her book *A Circle of Quiet*. There she talks about joy and what it means in terms of getting in touch with the child within us. "Far too many people misunderstand what *putting away childish things* means, and think that forgetting what it's like to think and feel and touch and smell and taste and see and hear like a three-year-old or a thirteen-year-old or a twenty-three-year-old means being grown up." But, she continues, "If I can retain a child's awareness of joy, and *be* fifty-one, then I will really learn what it means to be a grown-up."

I believe that we were made for joy, but we have forgotten what it smells like. We've forgotten what it looks like. We've forgotten how it sounds. I think of the little girl who sneaked into her baby sister's room and whispered, "Tell me about God. I'm forgetting."

This is a book about remembering God and the delights he wants to bring to your life. This is a book about joy. I welcome you to the Joyful Journey! Hold your hands out for the gift.

Joy, this gift to thy creation
Joy that flows from heaven's doors
Down upon the sons of Adam
Out to Eve's far distant shores.
Can a gift so rare and tender
Live in such a barren place?
If the heart will join the singing
Celebrate this gift of grace.

GETTING TO JOY

At the end of each chapter, I've included a few ideas about how you can enhance simple joys and open yourself more fully to God's love.

1. Even the bleakest childhood includes moments of wonder and joy. Throw a Joyful Moments party for a few close friends. Make it clear on the invitation that everyone will be given an opportunity to share a couple of special memories from childhood. Decorate the house with balloons and streamers. Serve ice cream and Jell-O and peanut butter and jelly sandwiches!

2. Make a "My Joyful Life" journal. Recapture as much as you can from your childhood. Write about special memories

and paste in old photographs, awards, school reports, or drawings.

3. Enjoy a few moments of wonder through the eyes of a child. I remember how much fun I had when I went with some of Pat Robertson's grandkids to see *Beauty and the Beast*. If you don't have children of your own or if they're all grown up, offer to take a friend's children for the day and enjoy life through their eyes.

4. Before you go to bed tonight, do one thing that will bring back a little joy from childhood. Have some cookies and milk or throw a duckie in your bath.

5. Take a trip or day outing that's more traditionally associated with children. Visit the zoo or the circus. Buy a children's book and curl up by the fire and read.

PART 2

SABOTAGING THE JOY

You do not look redeemed.
Friedrich Nietzsche

‍‍‍‍‍‍‍‍‍‍‍‍‍‍‍ꙮ

In her touching and insightful book *She Can Laugh at the Days to Come*, Valerie Bell tells a story that strikes a chord with me. She recounts her relationship with an arrogant but astute hairdresser named Trevor. I cringed as she described her treatment under his "professional" care, how he would not acknowledge her in any way as a fellow human being but treated her as little more than the spent locks of hair on the salon floor.

At the time Valerie was a devout Christian who perceived herself to be holy and above reproach. But one day as she sat in the salon, Trevor suddenly asked her, "Why are you so angry?"

Valerie was outraged by his question. But on reflection she saw that he had held a mirror up to her soul. She saw Trevor as worldly and mean and believed herself to be spiritual and above his shenanigans. She left that day not only with a new "do" but realizing she didn't look quite as redeemed as she thought. In time she realized she didn't feel quite as redeemed as she wished.

There are all sorts of little arrows that pierce our souls and let the joy leak out all over the floor. Understanding what those are and acknowledging them has helped me on my spiritual journey. Let's look at various ways we sabotage our joy—starting with the disappointments that drag us down.

21

CHAPTER 2

DISAPPOINTMENTS DRAG US DOWN

I cry to you for help, O LORD; in the morning my prayer comes before you. Why, O LORD, do you reject me and hide your face from me?

Psalm 88:13–14

$\sim$

I have never particularly enjoyed the process of being in the studio recording a new album. I see it as a necessary evil. I love to sing and I enjoy concerts, but being stuck in a stuffy room with a microphone, headphones, and a producer punching a button saying, "Do it again!" is not my idea of a good time. Buried deep in a pile of such mildly unpleasant memories lies a disappointment that haunted me for quite some time.

When I was eighteen I was part of a gospel group called Unity. We all lived in the same area on the west coast of Scotland and traveled on weekends to give concerts or be part of youth events. We became a big deal in our little neck of the woods and decided that it was time for us to make a record. I was one of three or four soloists in Unity, and two of the songs I sang were to be featured on the album. I was nervous but excited. *I bet this is how Barbra Streisand started*, I thought.

The musicians spent a few days laying down the tracks, and then it was time for the vocalists to step up to the plate. Brenda Bell went first and really nailed her song. She had a deep rich voice and sounded like a "redeemed" nightclub singer. I was next. My first song was the most contemporary on the album, and I was all ready to rock for Jesus. I sang it through a couple of times to warm up. I sounded good in the headphones with a lot of echo, and I felt confident enough to tell the engineer that I was ready for him to tape. I gave it all I had and waited for him to say that it was perfect and that they were going to keep it. He didn't. He asked me to do it again and again and again. After a frustrating couple of hours the producer asked me to come into the control room. "We're having a problem with your vocal," he said.

"What do you mean?" I asked. "Is it the mike?"

"No," he replied, "it's you. You can't seem to sing in tune."

I was devastated! I felt so embarrassed to be the one holding up the day's work. "Just give me a moment," I said. I went to the rest room and prayed a "help me" prayer. "I'm doing this for you, Lord," I reasoned. "Please help me sing in tune before the studio cat dies from the pain." I went back in to the control room and told the producer and engineer that I was ready now. I put my headphones back on with a new boldness. The music started and I went for it with great gusto. Before I was halfway through the first verse, I could tell from their expressions through the glass that God had not showed up in any miraculous way to assist me. It was awful. We tried for a few more hours until I ran out of the studio in tears, convinced that the engineer was an idiot, the producer was tone deaf, my career was over, and God hated music! I was so disappointed in myself.

Later that evening when things had calmed down, I was able to sing my song reasonably well before I crept off to bed with my tail between my legs.

Days like this one—some more disastrous, some less so—have a way of building one on top of another until we sometimes perceive our lives to be a series of disappointments. In others, in ourselves, in God. In life itself. We let disappointments sabotage our joy when we allow them to turn to anger, resentment, and guilt.

DISAPPOINTMENT WITH OTHERS

Our disappointment with others is easiest to pinpoint. Our first memory of a sibling pointing a finger at us and saying, "She did it." Memories of parents unleashing their irritations on us. A teacher blaming us for something we didn't do. I vividly remember my disappointment with my music teacher at school when I was sixteen. She was my hero. She took me under her wing and coached me for school productions and our local music festival. When it became clear to my mother that I had a great love for music and that God had gifted me with some ability, she signed me up for private voice lessons with our town's best voice coach, Harry Tweddle. I was very excited and couldn't wait to tell my teacher. I was completely unprepared for her response, which was anger. She felt I was betraying her by taking private lessons. She never spoke to me again for the remaining two years of high school. I was so upset that someone I admired so much would wipe me off her desk like yesterday's lesson.

Some of those old resentments fester into anger that is totally out of proportion to reality. I met a man who told me that he hadn't spoken to his twin in twenty years—and he couldn't remember why. Amazing.

Lies, whether spread maliciously or through exaggerated gossip, are especially painful, as they can be double betrayal. Not only is something said about us that's not true, but we are devastated when people we counted on believe the lie.

Not all the "hits" we receive are meant to be harmful. There can be a world of difference between what someone meant and what we heard. The fires of many rumors are built with little twigs that get piled on top of each other, and all it takes is a spark to ignite the bundle.

For some, a lifetime of disappointing relationships with Christians—having been hurt or bullied or misunderstood—leads to disillusionment with the church.

At the end of a morning worship service at which I was speaking, I innocently asked a stranger, "Is this your regular church?"

"I don't need it," she answered, referring to church in general. "My mom always said there are as many good Christians outside the church as in, and I agree! I just came to hear you," she continued. "I don't do church anymore. It's full of hypocrites."

Then she asked anxiously, "You don't believe you have to go to church to be a Christian?"

"No," I replied, "but it's like saying I don't have to bark to be a dog. It's what dogs do." Embarrassed by my poor illustration, I moved on. "The main reason I belong to a church is because it's God's idea."

"Yes," she admitted, "but that was written before the bunch at my church showed up!" We hugged and she hurried off before any "recruiters" could catch her.

I have a lot of sympathy for her position. Even we in the church disappoint each other all the time. Let's face it, we are a motley crew. We gossip and jockey for position in the name of Christian love. A dear friend has stopped attending church because he has been so hurt and has lost all faith in church leadership. We have sat over numerous cups of coffee and talked for hours about it, but his bottom line is that it's all a sham.

His disillusionment—and the disillusionment, pain, and anger I see in women I talk with across the country—disheartens me. I ache to see how these hurting people have allowed the disappointments they have suffered in the past to ruin their present—and their future.

I think of a scene in Dickens' *Great Expectations* between the unforgettable Miss Havisham and young Pip Pirrip. Pip has been summoned to the large and dismal home of Miss Havisham. He is terrified by the summons, as everyone knows Miss Havisham to be immensely rich and fiercely grim. He is greeted at the gate by a young girl and escorted along a dark corridor and left outside a door. Timidly he knocks and enters. In an armchair sits the strangest woman he has ever seen. She is dressed in white. A long veil trails on the floor, and there are faded flowers in her white hair. Her flesh is wrinkled and sallow like a ghastly waxwork figure. She speaks.

"Do you know what I touch here?" she says, laying her hands, one upon the other, on her left side.

"Yes, ma'am."

"What do I touch?"

"Your heart."

"Broken."

As a young woman Miss Havisham had been left at the altar on her wedding day, and now, decades later, sits still dressed in her wedding gown surrounded by her wedding breakfast, which is shrouded in cobwebs. A disturbing sight!

Do we do the same? I don't know what happened to the man who was supposed to have made Miss Havisham his bride, but we are led to assume that he went on with his life. It was she who was stuck. She couldn't come to terms with her betrayal, and life had stopped.

In his book *The Return of the Prodigal Son*, Henri Nouwen pinpoints the relationship between our resentments and disappointments and our inability to grasp hold of the joy of the Lord: "Not being able to enter into joy is the experience of a resentful heart. The elder son [in the parable of the Prodigal Son] couldn't enter into the house and share his father's joy. His inner complaint paralyzed him and let the darkness engulf him."

DISAPPOINTMENT WITH GOD

Sometimes it's easy for us to admit that we're disappointed with family members, friends, coworkers, or enemies. But some of us, if we were honest, would admit that we are disappointed with God. Having moved half a world away from their friends and family to serve God and then having been seriously let down by coworkers, a missionary recently wrote "home" to a confidante: "My husband and I are into this idea that God is out to get us. We feel betrayed and deserted."

Disappointment with God often starts with a question that can be finished a million different ways: If God loves me, why did ... happen? If God loves me, why am I in this marriage?

If God loves me, why did my child die? If God loves me, why am I suffering so much?

This is not a new song. The psalms are full of complaints. And 1 Kings 19 reveals the distress of Elijah, who's been a faithful witness for God and is now being chased by all the king's men. Elijah prays: "I have had enough, Lord. . . . I have been very zealous for the Lord God Almighty. The Israelites have rejected your covenant, broken down your altars, and put your prophets to death with the sword. I am the only one left, and now they are trying to kill me too" (vv. 4, 10). And Job—his life was decimated. Everything that made sense to him evaporated with the wind. His property was destroyed, his children died, his health was ruined. Job 3 starts with this commentary: Job "cursed the day of his birth." And it ends with Job saying, "I have no peace, no quietness; I have no rest, but only turmoil." How could God let this happen to him?

I recently had coffee with two women I'll call Samantha and Sarah. As a young woman Samantha's passion in life had been to be a good wife and mother. When a kind young man active in her church "romanced" her, she had been swept away. They shared common goals and dreams, or so she thought. They were married and had three children. Then one day he came home and planted the first bomb. "I don't love you anymore. There is someone else." She was stunned. For days she managed life as usual, as if her heart had been replaced by a computer chip. Then bomb number two. "I want you and the kids to move out till we can sort this out. Perhaps you can go and live with your mother."

She did it. She packed a bag for herself and another for the children, and they left their home. The warmth of their breath had hardly left their bedrooms before her husband had moved her replacement in.

"Why did you move out?" I asked.

"Because I knew God was going to change my husband's heart," she replied. "I believed that it was a statement of faith to others that my trust was not in what I saw but in whom I know. I fasted and prayed and waited for the phone call. I kept leading the choir at church and waited for the phone call. I told the kids not to worry, that God was working a miracle, and waited for the phone call. The call never came. What came in its place was divorce papers. I stood with them in my hands for what seemed like an hour in total disbelief."

That was twenty years ago. The children are now grown and gone and she lives alone. "What happened to you through those years?" I asked. "What happened to your faith in God?"

"At first I was devastated. Then I was angry. Then a cold numbness settled over me. It was years before I was able to let God comfort me. I felt as if he had abandoned me too."

Sarah's life also had not taken the turns she had hoped for. Approaching middle age, she has never married. "Are you angry with God?" I asked her.

"More let down, I think," she said. "I've tried so hard to do it God's way. I'm a forty-year-old virgin because I want God's best, but unless he hurries up, the crow's feet and spider veins will have taken over the building!" We all laughed at her joke, but it hurt too.

My heart aches for those I have talked to who are stunned by the outcome of their lives. I talked to a woman at a conference recently. "I am so lost," she said. "I've prayed over my kids since they were born. I claimed them for the kingdom and gave offerings to a television ministry in their names. The man said that if I sowed seed in faith that he would take my prayer request and my kids would be kept from ever falling prey to the devil." She stopped for a moment as her voice caught in her throat and tears poured down her face. "My daughter came home last week and told me she is pregnant. What went wrong?" She looked at me desperately as if I could somehow save the day. Right then I simply held her as she wept.

Many women I meet berate God or they berate themselves for their lack of faith, never thinking that maybe they need to back up and take a second look at life and God.

I say this with sorrow, but I see the contemporary church as being due for an outbreak of disappointment with God. Overdue. I think we have placed our hopes in an impostor, not in God. We castigate God or ourselves for our lack of faith, never thinking that it might be the formula that's at fault.

We erected a scriptural starting block—"I can do everything through him who gives me strength" (Philippians 4:13)—and then took off at breakneck speed to do all things and fell halfway through the race. Our generation sang "Bind Us Together" until we almost killed each other. We squandered faith on parking spots, and then ran out of faith when cancer hit the family. Like cheerleaders after the worst game of the season, we slipped quietly into our locker rooms mocked by the cheers still hanging in the air. What went wrong? Did we miss something?

We hear what we want to believe. As the Greek orator Demosthenes noted, "Nothing is so easy as to deceive one's self; for what we wish we readily believe."

It's human nature, as old as the prophets, to believe in the quick fix. Isaiah 30:9–11 talks of people "unwilling to listen to the LORD's instruction." They say, "Tell us pleasant things, prophesy illusions. Leave this way, get off this path, and stop confronting us with the Holy One of Israel!"

We live in a culture that wants "fast, now, new, painless, affordable." And we have made God into the image of our culture. In his book *Why Am I Afraid to Love?* John Powell, S.J., notes: "The book of Genesis says that God created man to his image and likeness. It seems that the most pervading heresy in all of Christian history has been this—that man has reversed Genesis—man has made God to his image and likeness."

We have become disappointed in God because we have erroneously come to believe that he is on *our* fast-track time schedule. We pray, "Lord, give me patience, and I need it *now!*" We bought into "fast, now, risk-free" Christianity. "Believe and you can have it, now! Claim it and drive around and pick it up." That sounds wonderful, but it's not biblical. God is not up for sale.

We're disappointed with God also because we have come to have faith in faith, rather than faith in God. As I travel across the country I have observed churches strewn with the wreckage of faith in faith; if we just had enough faith we could make God do what we want him to do.

But in and of itself a mountain of faith isn't going to move a mustard seed. It all depends on what your faith is in. Stuart Briscoe uses a wintertime image to illustrate that having more faith in a misconceived God doesn't work. He proposes that he could have great faith that the ice on a lake will hold him up and keep him from drowning. But if the ice is thin, his faith won't help him at all. He has faith in something of little substance, and he's in trouble. By contrast, he can have faith "as a grain of mustard seed" in a very thick layer of ice. With just a bit of faith he can step out onto that ice—and it will hold him. The ice is the critical factor—not his "great faith."

It's as though our generation arrogantly believes that we have God at our beck and call, that we understand God and his ways. But we don't, and we can't. In Isaiah 55:9, the Lord declares: "As the heavens are higher than the earth, so are my ways higher than your ways and my thoughts than your thoughts."

We sold our wares on a "do this and God will do that" platform and didn't stick around when it was returned to the lot as a lemon. Life with God under the new covenant of grace is not a quid pro quo relationship. We do not bargain with God: I'll do this for you; you do that for me. Yes, there may be painful consequences to our disobedience, and there may be blessing in obedience—but God does not owe us anything. It is all his grace. We are not equal partners sitting down at the table doing a deal. He pours his love out on us because that is who he is, not because we have earned it. We are called to "take up our cross every day and follow," and we do not get to pick the route.

As Terry Fullam says in *Living the Lord's Prayer*, "God is not a glorified genie in a bottle. Prayer is not tantamount to rubbing Aladdin's lamp to get him to come out and do our will."

"Sheila, you sound like a cynic," you say. "Don't you believe in miracles? Don't you have any faith?"

The truth is that I've never felt less cynical or been more excited about the journey of faith, but I want my faith to be placed in *God*—not a misconception of God.

DISAPPOINTMENT WITH OURSELVES

Another saboteur of joy is the many ways we are disappointed with ourselves. In short, we live with regrets that drag us down to the depths, sometimes to the depths of despair.

A biblical prayer critical to this whole book—"Restore to me the joy of your salvation" (Psalm 51:12)—was written by King David when he was dramatically confronted with his sin. Knowing the prohibition against adultery, he had slept with another man's wife. What's more, he'd then schemed to ensure that the soldier husband would be killed in battle. His intentional transgression of God's law jeopardized his relationship with God—and stole his joy. "I know my transgressions, and my sin is always before me," he declared (Psalm 51:3).

I was signing books recently and out of the corner of my eye noticed a woman still sitting in her seat sobbing into her hands. When everyone else had cleared the hall, I asked if I could sit down beside her. She said yes and then poured her heart out as tears ran like tiny rivers through her makeup. "Four years ago my husband and I were going through some pretty tough times financially. We had just begun to get on our feet a little when I discovered I was pregnant." She stopped for a moment and accepted the tissue I gave her. "I was horrified. We couldn't afford to have a baby. I knew that it would put incredible strain on my husband and on our marriage. I decided not to put that burden on him; I went by myself and had an abortion." She struggled to finish the last sentence as sobs racked her small frame again.

I took her hand in mine. "I'm so sorry," I said.

"What makes it unforgivable," she continued, "is that I'm a Christian, at least I claim to be. My husband is an elder in our church, and he doesn't know what I have done." She bent over in her pain—convinced her sin was beyond God's reach.

Many of us who have been Christians for years do not perceive ourselves as sinners of the first degree. We get up every morning intending to serve and please God, and yet ... with apostle Paul we do what we don't want to do. We miss the mark and then live in regret.

One of the greatest disappointments I have ever had is when I met myself. Our culture encourages us to "find ourselves." Well, I found myself, and it was a big letdown. Self-righteousness is a grotesque mask. For many years I carried around a large list in my soul. Every now and then I would bring it out, dust it off, and perhaps if it had been a good year add to it. It was my list of things I had never done. In my blindness people fell into two categories. Those who committed the big sins and those who did not. I rested smugly in the latter. If I heard of a friend or colleague who had fallen over one of the big rocks, I would do what I could to help, quietly thanking God that that would never happen to me.

In his grace and mercy, because he loves me, God committed himself to painting a portrait for me that showed me my true self. When you land in a psychiatric hospital, the gig is pretty well up. There's not much point in pretending that you're doing well—just check your new mailing address. But even that could have been a cowardly escape for me. "Poor me, I can't help this. I'm not well!" God would have none of it. What I saw in myself was that I was angry, controlling, and full of fear. Not a pretty picture. I wept for days over that new portrait. I wept to let go of the nice image of myself that I had polished for so long. I wept as I thought of how my arrogance must have bruised those I bumped into. I wept because I was so wrong when I thought I was so right.

I think of the apostle Paul—a Christian—admitting his own weakness: "What a wretched man I am! Who will rescue me from this body of death?" That question is followed by an exclamation: "Thanks be to God—through Jesus Christ our

Lord!" (Romans 7:24–25). Jesus is the only one who could rescue me from myself.

DISAPPOINTED WITH LIFE?

The first AA step is to admit you are powerless over alcohol. I suggest that this is the first step in dealing with our disappointments, to admit them and admit that we are powerless to change them. Admit you are needy, wounded by the past, hurt and confused by the present. Write a letter to God telling him what is disappointing in your relationship with him. God knows it all already, but it will help you to face what's true when you see it on paper. God knows about the secret abortion, the private fantasy life, the hatred you hold in your heart. It is only when we confess these things to God that he can fill the broken, empty places with his joy.

GETTING TO JOY

1. In a journal write down specific disappointments that keep you from experiencing the joy of your salvation. Write three lists: Disappointments with Others. Disappointments with God. Disappointments with Myself. Ask the Holy Spirit to bring everything to mind, and write as much as you need to.

2. Take your lists and bring them to the feet of Jesus. Read them to him and give them to him.

3. Find a trusted friend, voice your disappointments to her, and ask her to pray for you as you choose to face those disappointments and walk beyond them.

4. Find a symbolic way to "bury" your disappointments in Christ. Put them through a paper shredder or burn them or bury them in the yard.

5. On a new list, write down specific disappointments you have with your parent(s). For every disappointment, find and write two positive things about this parent.

6. Choose to dwell on these Scriptures:

Teach me, and I will be quiet; show me where I have been wrong. How painful are honest words!

Job 6:24–25

I know my transgressions, and my sin is always before me. . . . Create in me a pure heart, O God, and renew a steadfast spirit within me. Do not cast me from your presence or take your Holy Spirit from me. Restore to me the joy of your salvation and grant me a willing spirit, to sustain me.

Psalm 51:3, 10–12

I am in pain and distress; may your salvation, O God, protect me.

Psalm 69:29

Therefore, since we have been justified through faith, we have peace with God through our Lord Jesus Christ, through whom we have gained access by faith into this grace in which we now stand. And we rejoice in the hope of the glory of God. Not only so, but we also rejoice in our sufferings, because we know that suffering produces perseverance; perseverance, character; and character, hope. And hope does not disappoint us, because God has poured out his love into our hearts by the Holy Spirit, whom he has given us.

Romans 5:1–5

CHAPTER 3

DISTORTIONS
DEFINE US

*Lord, show me myself; let me respect and love my inner man,
and I shall be ready for the King of Glory to come in.*

Josephine Moffett Benton

Past disappointments can sabotage our joy. What's more,
they can make us misjudge the present. Because of what has
happened to us in the past, we perceive the present with distortion. I focus here on those disappointments having to do
with our self-definitions. *Who am I?* And ultimately by whose
gauge do I determine who I am?

One of Job's infamous friends, Eliphaz the Temanite, told
the suffering Job, "Is not your wickedness great? Are not your
sins endless? . . . You gave no water to the weary and you with-
held food from the hungry" (Job 22:5, 7). Yet we know from
what the Bible tells us that God considered Job to be a righteous and holy man. Eliphaz's words were not at all true.

Job did not believe his friend's words. But far too many
of us know the influence that other people—family or friends
or enemies—have on who we perceive ourselves to be. We
believe the wrong voices. Let's look at a few of the most common distortions of ourselves that I hear among Christians, especially women.

THE MYTH OF THE SUPER WOMAN

Many of us are discontent with who we are and what we have because the media tells us we can and should "have it all." The women's movement swept across the country whistling a tune that was like a siren's song for many who felt unfulfilled and abandoned. We bought into the picture of the woman who could "have it all," but the paint wasn't even dry on that theory before it became clear that no one is built to have it all or be it all or do it all. Instead of facing that reality, we get depressed or feel guilty.

This is especially true for mothers of young children. As a culture we worship monetary success. Even as a church we see that as a sign of God's blessing. We want the good jobs that will bring in good money—and give us some professional respect. But we also want to be there with and for our children. And, let's be honest, our culture doesn't put much value on the demanding, nurturing role of raising children. I have strong memories of coming home from school every day and my mother being there. I didn't always want to talk, but it was good to know that she was there. We would have had more money if she had gone out to work, but we had her and that was a surer foundation than any new outfit or gadget. For many women today that's not possible. Single moms struggle to raise children alone. Every mom struggles with hard choices—and most struggle with a discontent that they don't measure up to the image of a successful woman; they sink a little lower every day.

How is the woman who is still awake at midnight folding clothes and tucking little notes into lunch pails to measure her life? How does the childless woman, desperately wishing for a baby, measure her life? Too often any of us—all of us—measure our worth by external factors—who some magazine or speaker or even pastor tells us we're supposed to be.

THE CURSE OF SHAME

But I often see a deeper issue in terms of the lies we believe about who we are. One of the greatest barriers to joy is shame. Shame tells us that we are no good.

I was sharing my story at a church in California, and at the end of the service a man waited to talk to me. He must have been in his early fifties, smartly dressed, apparently successful. "When you talked about shame today," he said, "you were talking about me."

"What do you mean?" I asked.

"When I was a young boy my mother told me that she should never have had me. Having one more child ruined her health."

He stopped and the pain in his face was palpable.

"I've worked so hard all these years," he continued, "but I just can't shake the fact that I was a mistake, that my very existence is wrong."

This man was allowing his mother's disappointments and distortions to control his self-identity. We prayed together, and after he left I wondered how many others walking around among us feel at the very core of their being that they are a mistake—not because of their actual wrongdoing, but because they carry someone else's burden as their own.

Guilt and shame feel very much alike. Guilt tells us that we have *done* something wrong. Shame tells us that we *are* something wrong. To the best of our abilities we can make amends when we *do* something wrong, but if we feel we *are* something wrong, what then? People who live with shame feel that no matter *what* they do, it is wrong.

I was a child when my father was changed forever, as the result of a blood clot that traveled to his brain and decimated who he had always been to me—a loving, caring man. My last memory of him was his looking at me with intense rage. I couldn't understand why the person who had loved me so much now seemed to hate me. What had I done to change the look in his eyes? What had he seen in me that was so unlovable? For a long time this affected my relationship with God and with others. Shame was my companion. In my childish reasoning I concluded that it was my fault that my father hated me, and that if he hated me, others would hate me too if they really knew who I was. So I tried to be perfect. I tried to never disappoint anyone. I longed to be loved for who I really was, and yet the thought of revealing who I really was and what I really thought was terrifying. What if at my most vulnerable I was rejected?

As a teenager I used to hate it when the phone rang. My first thought was "who is it and what have I done?" Considering that my most besetting teenage sin was borrowing my sister's sweaters, it was an unreasonable fear. As I entered adulthood the stakes became a lot higher. I did my best to live an honorable life, but insecurity crept all over me like ivy on an old house. For too long I lived externally a very public life but was internally isolated because I felt so worthless.

COMPENSATING CAPERS

How do some of us compensate for this negative self-image?

Many of us choose to live "noisy" lives. We don't enjoy the companionship of ourselves, so we turn up the car stereo or tune in our favorite television show. When it's noisy, you don't have to think. Not when you live vicariously through characters on TV or in paperback novels.

And many of us try to be someone we're not. When I was growing up there was always someone else I thought I'd rather be. I remember a girl in my class at school called Laura Bannerman. She was very beautiful and poised. She was confident where I was clumsy. I used to watch her and attempt to emulate the way she moved or laughed, but it never really worked. Even if it had worked it would have been a hollow victory. People would have been seeing "Sheila Walsh Does Laura Bannerman."

We're convinced that we'd be accepted—by others, by God, by ourselves—if we had more flash.

Or maybe if we were more beautiful.

When we moved into our home in Franklin, Tennessee, I decided to sort through some of my "stuff." It was amazing what had been thrown into a cupboard just in case it was ever needed. "What's this?" Barry said as he opened a box containing a row of what resembled six dead hamsters.

"It's my 'luxurious hair,'" I replied.

I had fallen prey to one more "We can make your life better" TV offer. It promised immediate and glorious long hair by pinning hair pieces under your own hair. I had tried it, but it made me look like a cocker spaniel. In that sorting spree I also found two "Abdominizers" and a host of other items that had promised they would make me be someone more fit or beautiful than I was.

Was this effort to be more beautiful vain *pride* on my part? I think not. For centuries the church has named pride as one of the seven "deadly" sins. But I can see that sometimes what looks like pride is self-loathing in disguise.

I had a friend who could not face the fact that he was losing his hair. It had begun to thin when he was in his early twenties. He knew his family history. By age forty-five his dad was completely bald, and the prospects of "looking like my dad" were too frightening for him to face. My friend, in his early thirties, had one faithful patch that kept growing. Trying to hold on to his youth, he gave that patch of hair the run of his whole head. He combed it over, under, and around and then sprayed it down with the beauty salon's version of super glue in a can. It looked ridiculous.

Not willing to face the reality of what he perceived to be imperfection, my friend was tied up in knots, worried, and fretful—and missing out on the joy of today. Who was he? From all appearances it seemed he defined himself by his hair: *I am bald—and ashamed of it.*

My friend's unsuccessful attempts at hiding his nearly bare head seem an apt analogy for many of us in the church. We try hard to compensate for what we don't have or feel. We try to trick ourselves and others into thinking that we've got something that we don't really have: victory in Christ. And we don't have that victory—that joy—because we don't have a solid biblical understanding of who we are in him.

TRYING TO PROVE OURSELVES WORTHY

I see too many joyless Christian women who are depressed and exhausted in their efforts to prove themselves worthy of space on the planet or space in the hearts of family, friends, or God himself.

A couple of years ago I received a sad letter from a woman who had read my book *Honestly*. She admired my courage in getting help for clinical depression. She too suffered from extreme depression, but would not go for help because she thought admitting her need would cause her to lose her church leadership role. Then one line really struck me: "I feel that as long as I am helping others God can see how much I love him and if I stopped that I would have nothing to give." I could have cried as I read those words. I understand the lure of ministry— but I've also learned that it often takes us away from real relationship with Christ. We can give and give and give, but we'll never prove ourselves or our ministry worthy to God.

I remember seeing a woman walking out of a Women of Faith conference. "I give up!" she said.

I could see from the look on her face that she meant it. She seemed so perturbed and out of place, considering the smiles of the other women who were streaming out of the arena. "What's up?" I asked. "Didn't you enjoy the conference?"

"Enjoy it! That's a joke. I never got to hear one single speaker."

"What happened?" I asked. "Did you lose your ticket?"

"No, I finally lost my mind!"

I pulled out a chair from behind my book table and invited her to sit down. "Tell me about it," I said.

"Well," she began, "I brought a large group of ladies from our church. I organized the whole thing by myself, booked the hotel, the whole nine yards. I'm always doing something for other people, and all I'd like is a little recognition, a little appreciation, but instead I run around like a chicken with my head cut off taking care of everyone else's problems. And then one lady had the cheek to say to me that I should have heard Patsy Clairmont because I need a little joy in my life!" She stopped for breath, and it seemed to me that we could have run the lights from the steam that was shooting out of her ears.

What was she trying to prove to whom?

Basing a life—and a witness—on our own attempts to prove ourselves has a way of perpetuating the negative and inaccurate image we hold of ourselves.

No matter how hard we strain toward a goal, we fall two inches short. We can never "jump high enough" to satisfy the "must do" that drives us—that defines us. Even if we meet a realistic goal, we simply convince ourselves that we failed. This time just like last time. And the cycle continues:

I am a loser. (This always happens to me!)

I am a nobody. (No one ever treats me with any respect!)

I am hopeless. (I'll never be able to overcome this sin.)

I am not a success. (People think I'm a success, but I know I'm a fake.)

The voices in your soul that claim you are worthless, that you will never change, that there is no hope for you—these are not messages from God but from the enemy of our souls who wants to keep us defeated in heart and mind. In Hebrew Satan means "accuser," and Revelation 12:10 specifically calls him "the accuser of our brothers."

John 8:44 describes Satan as "the father of lies." The implication of those words is often lost in the shuffle of our emotions. We believe his lies, sometimes because we get some perverse pleasure in walking in the darkness. (Sometimes the light hurts our eyes!) Sometimes we're afraid to walk in and toward the truth. The price of "letting go" seems too high.

Remember the woman I just described who had come to a Women of Faith conference but missed the whole program? We talked for a while that evening. I suggested that it was time she stopped and reassessed what she was doing and why. In the end, I said, "You might like yourself better. You might catch a glimpse of the joy of the Lord." She looked at me with sad eyes, as if I were selling something that cost ten dollars and she had only ten cents.

In *A Grief Observed*, C. S. Lewis tells of an experience his wife had—before they married. One morning she felt "haunted" by what she felt was God "demanding her attention." Lewis continues, "Not being a perfected saint, she had the feeling that it would be a question, as it usually is, of some unrepented sin or tedious duty. At last she gave in—and faced him. But the message was 'I want to give you something,' and instantly she entered into joy."

STOP!

I hear stories of exhausted, depleted women who are tired of trying to prove themselves, and I want to say *stop*. It doesn't work. Your struggle is as futile as a fly struggling against fly paper. As long as you hold onto basic faulty definitions of who you are, you won't find the joy. As long as you try to win God's approval, or prove to him that you're "worthy" of anything, the joy will be just out of your reach.

I tell them my own story and how I have changed. Initially I didn't do it voluntarily. I simply collapsed under the weight of my self-loathing. What liberation can be found in the ashes of a life, when you finally discover who God is, who you are, and who God wants you to be.

And there's something wonderfully circular about the joy of our salvation. When we find it, it becomes our strength—maybe even our definition. As Nehemiah told his people: "The joy of the LORD is your strength" (Nehemiah 8:10).

GETTING TO JOY

1. Facing what doesn't work is the first step toward finding out what does. My "luxurious" hair didn't work, nor did anything else I tried to do to be "worthy." Write down the things you do to validate who you are in your relationship with your husband, friends, family, church, and God.

2. Write in your journal what you think makes you loved and valued by God and others.

3. Robert Burns, a poet from my hometown in Scotland, wrote:

   O wad some Power the giftie gie us
   To see ourselves as others see us.

   Ask a couple of trusted friends for feedback as to what they love and value in you and compare this list to what you have written in exercise 2.

4. Ask your parent(s) for a letter telling you what it is about you that makes you special to them. (What do they appreciate about you?) I will always treasure a letter that my mom wrote to me after I had been in the psychiatric hospital telling me how much she loved and valued me and why.

5. On the next rainy day or when you have a couple of free hours, take a pile of magazines and cut out pictures that remind you in some way of your life. Make a collage.

6. Choose to meditate on these Scriptures:

   Jesus said, "It is not the healthy who need a doctor, but the sick."
                                                    Matthew 9:12

   What, then, shall we say in response to this? If God is for us, who can be against us?
                                                    Romans 8:31

   If anyone is in Christ, he is a new creation; the old has gone, the new has come!
                                                    2 Corinthians 5:17

CHAPTER 4

FEARS
CLOUD THE FUTURE

For as children tremble and fear everything in the blind darkness, so we in the light sometimes fear what is no more to be feared than the things children in the dark hold in terror and imagine will come true.

Lucretius

Lord, I am afraid.
I'm afraid of being alone.
I'm afraid of being with anyone else.
I'm afraid of failing.
I'm afraid of trying.
I'm afraid to change.
I'm afraid I'll never change.
Lord, I'm afraid.
Help me.

We've looked at joy saboteurs grounded in past disappointments and present self-definitions. Let's turn to our outlook of the future. How does fear and anxiety cloud the horizon?

Let me state the obvious about fear: Like freedom, fear is a state of mind. I know people who are terrified of boarding airplanes. But I love to fly. Barry loves to hide under the covers when it's cold, but I panic because I'm claustrophobic. I used to collect white mice when I was ten years old, but my mother had a fit if I brought them into the house. Our fears can vary as much as our personalities.

And another obvious characteristic of fear: Our fears of the future are colored by the disappointments and distortions that have layered upon us and within us up to the present moment. We have so many layers to our lives that we get lost under the folds.

EXAGGERATIONS OF THE IMAGINATION

Some of our fears are irrational. Jeremy Taylor, a seventeenth-century Anglican bishop, said, "A great fear, when it is ill-managed, is the parent of superstition." The awareness of that "expansion" of reality underlies some ethnic proverbs. The Jewish Talmud says, "He who has been bitten by a snake is frightened by a rope." And there's an African version: "He who is bitten by a snake fears a lizard."

When I was a child I was frightened by a boy in my class who jumped out at me from behind a wall. He was wearing a hideous Halloween mask. From that moment till now I have an unreasonable fear of people in masks. A few years ago I was in Tampa, Florida, doing a concert for a church youth group. At the end of the evening we all went out for pizza at Chuck E. Cheese's (Chuck being the name of a large costumed mouse). I was heading back to my table when I felt a hand on my shoulder. I turned around, thinking it was one of the kids, and came face-to-face with a six-foot mouse. I got such a fright that I threw my pizza and Coke all over his furry costume. I was humiliated and Chuck was soaked. We all laughed about it later, but it ruined my evening because it touched on such a raw nerve.

The expansion of the imagination can steal your joy faster than electricity responds to the flick of a switch.

OUR NUMBER-ONE FEAR

One poll, cited in *No More Fears* by Douglas Hunt, showed that both men and women named "loss of control" as their number-one fear. This fear, like most, starts with a question that is not unhealthy in itself, but it is unhealthy when it is chronically negative. "What if?" What if I have a car accident? What if I make a fool of myself? What if I never get a promotion? What if I never have a child? What if I fall off the stage?

My friend Brennan Manning says that this line of thinking can rule one's life. When that happens you take out "a second mortgage in the house of fear."

I can see that many of my fears have been that number-one fear of loss of control, especially when it comes to my career as a performer, interviewer, and public speaker. I remember speaking in Tulsa at a Women of Faith conference in 1997. I really wanted the evening to go well, as I had some friends there and I was excited for them to experience the joy of the weekend. The night before I got no sleep. Christian was teething and when he finally fell asleep, the wedding party that had been celebrating in the lobby bar when we arrived moved into the room next to us and belted out songs they certainly didn't learn in Sunday school! In the morning I was exhausted. I decided that I'd feel better if I took more time than normal doing my hair, so I tried out a slightly different look. Just before we left for the arena, Barry, who'd been at the venue all day, came in and asked me what on earth I'd done to my hair. I told him he was an insensitive moron and jumped back into the shower. *Oh well*, I thought, *at least I have my lovely new white suit.* Five minutes before I went on stage, Christian threw up an entire jar of carrots on my jacket, and I had nothing else to change into. All illusion of being even vaguely in control dripped off me with the carrots. Going on stage that evening was particularly daunting.

And, since I've become a mother, that fear of loss of control has gone to a new depth: fearing for the well-being of my child. With the delight of motherhood came a vulnerability that I have never experienced before. And it hit me full-force just days after Christian's birth. What looked to me like a Bermuda tan the doctor said was jaundice. He explained that because the baby had arrived three weeks early, his liver was not quite ready. They took some blood and told us to take him out in the December California sunshine for as much of the day as possible. We were to bring Christian back to the doctor the next day; if the "billirubin levels" hadn't improved they would arrange for lights to be delivered to our home. I held him as they took blood from his tiny foot. He cried so hard it almost broke my heart.

We went home. Hours later the doctor called and told us to get Christian into pediatric intensive care within the hour, because something else had "shown up" in his blood. We threw a few things in the car, including the dog to drop off at the kennel, not knowing how long we would be at the hospital. Barry ran into the kennel with Bentley, leaving me alone with Christian and feeling absolutely desperate.

"Please don't do this!" I cried out loud to God, tears rolling down my face. "Please don't take my little boy." If someone had walked up to me at that point and said, "Sheila, will you relinquish your son to the Lord?" I would have said "No." I'm sorry, Abraham. I was so afraid that if I said yes, God would take him.

In thirty minutes Barry and I were being told how to scrub up (for ten minutes!) and how to put masks and gowns on. We were escorted into intensive care, to unit D-5. It all seemed so clinical. But this was *our* tiny baby lying in that plastic incubator. When a nurse said they would need to tape a patch over his eyes, I gasped, "But he'll be afraid."

"No, he won't," she said kindly. "Remember, he's kind of familiar with the dark."

A doctor explained the problem—that Christian's white blood count was off. "It's not leukemia," he said, "but there are other things we need to look for."

The next morning the doctor told us there had been a mistake and that apart from a little jaundice there had never been anything wrong with Christian. As we drove home with our baby boy, strong images were burned into my mind. The look on the faces of others parents in the unit, the tiny baby in the room next to Christian's who labored hard for every breath, the fear that grabbed my heart when an alarm went off over our incubator and the relief when the nurse told me it was from another room, my feelings of guilt that I was glad it was another baby. I'd never felt such primal emotions. I'd never felt so desperate, so afraid, so small, so out of control. *How can such joy and terror come wrapped in the same gift?* I wondered. As I tucked him into his blue bassinet by our bed, I said to him, "Okay, here are the ground rules. You can go out and play when you are twenty if you wear protective gear, and you may start dating when you're thirty-five!" His dad came and stood behind me laughing at my speech. Once more we placed Christian—as well as ourselves—in God's hands.

OUR NUMBER-TWO FEAR

The fear survey that showed loss of control as the prevailing fear for men and women showed rejection as the number-two fear of women. (Rejection ranked fourth for men.) I can see this in the women I talk with. We want love, attention. We are afraid we will be abandoned, left out in the cold.

The Hebrew notion of hell is not so much fire and brimstone as it is being alone, forgotten from memory, abandoned. On the other end of the spectrum, heaven is perceived in terms of a marriage.

When I think of the fear of being alone, rejected, abandoned, I think of Barbara, a nurse I met when I was sixteen and volunteering at a hospital for the elderly one night a week. She was single, about fifty years old, and great fun. The patients loved her and so did I. But one evening she told me that she would be gone by Christmas. I was surprised, because I knew she loved her job. "Why, Barbara?" I asked. "Are you moving on to another hospital?"

She looked at me for a few seconds. "You're too young for this stuff, kid," she said.

"What do you mean?" I asked. "Tell me why you're going."

"Because this will be me in twenty years lying here with no hope, no dignity, no privacy. I can't stand it anymore. So I'm leaving now to enjoy a few years of peace before I find myself in one of these beds."

Barbara echoed the fears of many in our society of ending up alone. Career women, divorced women, single women, unhappy women, knowing that a nice home is not enough if you sit alone. We live with a fear that we will somehow be abandoned and rejected.

On a recent trip to New York I had dinner with Jim Bakker. We were staying in the same hotel, speaking at the same conference. As he shared some of his memories and impressions of his time in prison for fraud, one story in particular stood out to me. He shared a cell with a young man incarcerated for particularly brutal crimes. Jim described him as a "solid wall of a guy," the kind you wouldn't mess with. But at night, in his sleep, this young man cried out for his mother. Was the tough-guy image just a facade hiding a frightened boy, looking for the security of a mother's arms?

ADAM'S FEAR AND OURS

Some of the fear we live with is as old as Adam and Eve's fear after their fateful fall: the fear of being found out and found wanting. After eating of the forbidden fruit, Adam knew something was wrong. Not being able to undo his act, he tried to cover himself—with fig leaves. And then in the evening, when God came walking through Eden for a conversation, God asked Adam a telling question. "Where are you?"

What did Adam answer? "I was afraid because I was naked; so I hid" (Genesis 3:10).

And God's response? "Who told you that you were naked?" (verse 11). Hadn't Adam been created naked? Something had happened to make Adam feel he needed to fear—and hide.

Ever since Adam our guilt and an added burden of shame loaded on over the generations have caused us to live in fear of being found out and being found wanting—like my teenage fear of the phone ringing and someone "catching" me. I think much of our unhealthy fear is based in our guilt or our shame. Because of our past actions (ways we disappointed ourselves or God) and our present distortions, we fear what might be in the future.

We're afraid we don't and won't measure up. And that fear causes us to hide not only from God but from others. An old African American spiritual talks of Adam but speaks for all of us: "Adam's in the garden pinning leaves." That line shows the absurdity of thinking that our "pinning" is really doing any good. Satan must delight in his ability to keep us hiding from each other in the church—hiding from each other in the little isolation units we have built around ourselves.

Recently a pastor's wife told me that she has struggled with depression for several years but feels unable to get help because she doesn't want to let her husband and the church down. I saw loneliness and sadness in her eyes. I heard her silent scream for help that she longs for but is afraid of.

I thought of another woman I had talked to the previous evening. She threw her arms around me as would someone who had been pulled out of the icy waters of the Atlantic after the *Titanic* sank. "Thank you!" she said. "Thank you for helping me find the courage to get help. I've waited a long time, terrified to voice my fears even to myself. I've wished I were dead, but tonight you stood on stage and told my story, and you're still standing." She hugged me again and she was gone.

Our fear becomes like the millstone that pulls us under the water. Our silence adds weight to the stone. In his book *Putting Your Faith to Work*, John Redhead calls fear "Private Enemy Number One." I see his phrase as a play on words, because fear has such a power to keep us in our own private worlds. Hiding behind our "leafy aprons," we try to keep our sin and pain and shame such a secret. And the effort it takes to keep the "secret" only makes the pain worse.

In 1996 the British film *Secrets and Lies* was nominated for best film in the Academy Awards. What a powerful story. It's my favorite kind of movie, human drama, a slice of life. The main characters—a husband and wife and the man's sister—live in private emotionally tortured worlds, hugging their pain close to their chests. They have various sources of pain—infertility, old resentments, and misunderstandings that have led to distrust, and an unacknowledged illegitimate child. But it's clear that that pain is exacerbated by the great effort it takes to hide it—for fear of what others would think or say if the secrets and lies and misunderstandings were openly confronted.

A young woman—the grown illegitimate daughter—tiptoes into the family scene and breaks down the walls that separate this group that has been living a hellish isolation from each other. At one point the infertile wife nearly cowers in the corner, the emotional pain oozing from the pores in her face. Her husband is urging her to admit (to his sister) that she is incapable of having a child. Her husband confronts her: "Just tell her the truth. Why can't you tell her?"

Because of the isolation caused by fear. Too many of us—even Christians—are prisoners of our secrets, prisoners of the lies we've lived with or chosen to believe. They say that a secret has no power once it is told, but when it is quietly kept it is a brutal taskmaster, *the lord of solitary confinement.* Why secrets? Why would those who are "children of the light" spend so much time alone in the darkness?

LOOSENING THE NOOSE

In his book *Essentials*, Jean Toomer uses a great simile to describe the power fear can have—if we let it: "Fear is a noose that binds until it strangles." It strangles the joy from our life. It strangles any hope we have for a bright future. It strangles our ability to step out and take the risks that will open up healthy relationships with others.

That noose can be cut and we can be set free.

But, you say, I've gotten used to the feel of the noose. I was talking to a group of women about fear and the place it occupies in our lives. One woman said, "Fear is what's holding me together. Without it I'd be like a sweater. I'd unravel." We all laughed, but we knew there was some truth to her words. Fear was half of the structure of her life, and she was afraid (there's that word again) of what would hold her together if it were gone.

You may be afraid to let go of your fear. If so, I again challenge you just to stop. Take a deep breath—and let it out. Let that breath be your very first step toward letting go. Look at one positive "what if." What if you chose to cut the noose? What if you chose to take one hopeful step that in so doing you could know the joy of the Lord?

GETTING TO JOY

1. Take a good look at your life. In your journal, write down what you perceive to be the three greatest fears that cloud your heart and your horizon.

2. Search your Bible for three verses to counter those fears. Write the verses down on cards and put them on your refrigerator. For example, "Peace I leave with you; my peace I give you. I do not give to you as the world gives. Do not let your hearts be troubled and do not be afraid" (John 14:27).

3. Bring your journal reflections before God. Ask yourself the question that Christ asked of the man at the pool of Siloam, "Do you want to get well?" (John 5:6). Are you willing to let go of your fears?

4. In *Vitamins for Your Soul*, Traci Mullins and Ann Spangler say, "It's natural to want to deny or run from feelings and thoughts that make us uncomfortable. Next time you feel like running, defy your natural instinct and turn instead to face whatever is going on inside you. Try saying out loud,

with gentleness, 'Welcome fear. Hello, bitter memory. What do you want to say to me?' Then listen."

5. Do one small thing today that you are afraid of. As you step out in faith, think of this Scripture: "Have no fear of sudden disaster or of the ruin that overtakes the wicked, for the LORD will be your confidence" (Proverbs 3:25–26).

PART 3

RESTORING
THE JOY

Restore to me the joy of your salvation and grant me a willing spirit, to sustain me.

Psalm 51:12

To get a handle on a few saboteurs to joy, we've looked at our past, present, and future. But I think it's obvious that life—today—isn't that easily compartmentalized. We want and need joy today, but our today is tainted by yesterday and by our view of tomorrow.

So this part, about restoring joy, isn't so clearly organized in terms of our own past, present, future. It starts and ends with the One who called himself I AM—meaning "I WAS, I AM, I WILL BE." He is the unchanging, everlasting God.

Many children who grew up in the church learned a spelling song, which proposed that J-O-Y was an acronym for Jesus-Others-You, as if this line-up were the secret of knowing the joy of the Lord.

Ultimately, I agree! That's why I'm turning the topic to God and who he is.

But there's really no easy or catchy 1-2-3 formula for appropriating joy. Joy happens in us as God restores us, teaching us to abide in him as he works in and through us.

CHAPTER 5

JOY: FRUIT YOU WERE MEANT TO BEAR

God can't give us happiness and peace apart from himself
because there is no such thing.

C. S. Lewis, *Mere Christianity*

﹥ߡ

In December 1993 if you had asked me if I knew Barry
Pfaehler, I would have said, "Yeah, sure I do." We'd met
on June 25, 1993. I remember it so well because it was his birthday. I was a guest on a television talk show on the West Coast
and Barry was director of programming for the network. I don't
believe in love at first sight, but there was something that happened between us that was overwhelming. We just stared at
each other. Eventually I asked him if there was somewhere I
could go to fix my makeup, and he showed me into his office.
He sat on a chair behind his desk just gawking at me as I
attempted to ignore him and get my lipstick on my lips and not
my chin. He asked if he could call and take me out to lunch.
I said yes.

I spent hours getting ready. We had decided on the phone
to make it dinner instead of lunch, and I wanted to look great
but also as if I hadn't given it much thought. We had a wonderful evening. We had dinner in an Italian restaurant in
Laguna Beach and then went to see *Sleepless in Seattle*. It was
perfect.

In December we were still dating. Did I know him? Yes, we liked the same food and the same kind of movies. We felt the same about so many things. I loved his honesty and kindness, and the fact that I almost fainted every time he walked into a room!

A year later, in December 1994, I married him—and suddenly I thought I hadn't known him at all. Relationship—intimate relationship—made all the difference.

Today I know him—and love him—in a way I never did before our wedding in Charleston, South Carolina. I can tell when his back is sore or what tie he'll like, when to hug him and when to give him space. I still could faint when he walks into a room. Our relationship has grown and continues to grow, and out of the depth of that relationship, we have been graced with the precious fruit of our love, our son, Christian. Sometimes when he laughs I see Barry. Sometimes when he stares off into the distance I see myself in the intensity of his gaze.

Christian is the fruit of our love and of our committed, ever-growing relationship—in much the same way that joy is the fruit of our relationship with God.

THE FRUIT OF THE SPIRIT IS JOY

The apostle Paul says that joy is a fruit of our life in and with the Spirit of God: "The fruit of the Spirit is love, joy, peace, patience, kindness, goodness, faithfulness, gentleness and self-control" (Galatians 5:22–23).

What does that mean? It means joy is not something that you can buy or chase. You can't get it from a book or a conference. You can't absorb it as if by osmosis by hanging out with people who seem to have it. You can spend your life trying to eliminate all pain and stress from your world in the vain hope that joy will take its place. It won't. You can beg for it, pray for it, bargain for it to no avail. Because joy comes only when you live in relationship with the source of joy.

I spoke of Christian being the fruit of my marriage to Barry. Of course fruit is most often seen as a garden image—

fruit trees, grape vines, berry bushes, tomato plants growing fruit as they are nourished through the cords of the plant. The *Living Bible* gives a graphic version of another garden image: "It was God, not we, who made the garden grow in your hearts" (1 Corinthians 3:6).

Joy is also critical to another "fruity" biblical passage, John 15. Jesus says, "I am the true vine and my Father is the gardener. . . . Remain in me, and I will remain in you. No branch can bear fruit by itself; it must remain in the vine. Neither can you bear fruit unless you remain in me" (vv. 1, 4). The metaphor ends with Jesus saying: "I have told you this so that my joy may be in you and that your joy may be complete" (v. 11).

I can't say that I know much about gardening. My husband and I are plant killers. We recently purchased two cedar trees to put in large pots on either side of our front door. For the first couple of days we watered them faithfully, and then Barry's mom and dad came to stay. His dad is to plants what the cavalry was years ago to wagon trains headed for the West—a welcome sight! For the two weeks he was with us, Bubsie Pfaehler loved our plants, and they smiled in deep gratitude. But then he went home. And the cedars died. So much for my knowledge of plants. But I do know that fruit doesn't grow on a branch when the branch is not connected to the vine.

This vine-branch image of Jesus' indicates that we have a choice as to whether or not we remain in the vine. In a little book *The Way of the Sevenfold Secret*, written eighty years ago to explain Christianity to Sufi Muslims, Lilias Trotter explains it well: "One danger is that we may let go our hold: that is why Christ says 'abide in me.'. . . 'Abide in me' means that we must keep our hold on Christ: '[And I] abide in you' means that we must let him lay hold and keep hold of us." So that we may bring forth the fruit of the Spirit. So that our joy may be full!

I think of the Old Testament story of the spies who explored the Promised Land while the children of Israel were still wandering in the desert. In the Valley of Eshcol they found and harvested a cluster of grapes that was so big it took two men to carry it on a pole (Numbers 13). That must have been some well-fertilized bunch of grapes! Maybe someone got carried away with the Miracle Grow? If God is the source of our joy, the size of the joy he wants to grow in us is "inexpressible and glorious" (1 Peter 1:8). Watch out for the amazing harvest!

Don't think that I'm saying that bearing joy means walking around with a smile slapped on your face morning till night. There is a difference between joy and happiness. As Phillip Keller says in *A Gardener Looks at the Fruits of the Spirit*, "Happiness is extremely vulnerable. It is insecure and unsure. At best it is established on unreliable, unpredictable ground." Many things outside of ourselves can make us happy. Joy, however, is an inside thing that doesn't depend on circumstance. It's above and beyond the good and bad that meet us on our paths. It is within us.

Happiness depends on circumstance; joy depends on relationship—our relationship with God.

THE TRUTH ABOUT GOD

Scripture is full of insights about who God is. And whole books are written about knowing God, who is perfect, righteous, holy, eternal, omnipotent, and more.

Here I deal with three aspects of God tied to the three virtues listed in 1 Corinthians 13:13: "Now these three remain: faith, hope and love." They "remain" (or "abide," as translated in the King James Version), reminiscent of Jesus' instruction that we "remain" or "abide" in him.

God Is Love

The father of lies does not want God's children to grasp the full meaning of those three powerful words: "God is love" (1 John 4:8).

I think we just don't get it. *No matter where you are, no matter who you are, God loves you.* I pray that a year from now or five years from now I will be a more godly woman than I am today, but I know that God then will not love me one bit more than he does right at this minute. Stop for a moment and take a look at yourself in the mirror. Allow this truth to wash over your face: God loves me with all of heaven right now, just as I am: gray hairs, smeared mascara, telltale lines, and all.

Then take a peek inside and allow this truth to wash through your heart: God loves me just the way I am—quick tempered, procrastinating, envious, or gossipy. He loves me.

Scripture uses male pronouns for God, and Jesus referred to his Father in heaven, and yet we are often quick to overlook Scriptures that refer to the motherlike love of God. Through Isaiah God says, "As a mother comforts her child, so will I comfort you" (66:13).

The apostle Paul uses very intimate language when he writes to the church in Thessalonica. "We were gentle among you, like a mother caring for her little children. We loved you so much that we were delighted to share with you not only the gospel of God but our lives as well, because you had become so dear to us" (1 Thessalonians 2:7–8).

I've heard people say that having a child of your own helps you to better understand the depth of God's love for his children, but I had no idea just how powerful a parable my son's life would be to me. I love him intensely and yet I know that my love is at best a poor shadow of God's love for me. When he laughs I laugh too. When he cries I hold him and comfort him. When he's scared I let him bury his face in my neck just as you and I are invited to bury our faces in the mane of the Lion of Judah.

When I walk into a room now and Christian is there, all I want to do is hold him. If I've been working upstairs on my computer and come down for a cup of tea, and he's awake, I would see him before I would see an elephant standing beside him. My heart has been permanently enlarged. I don't love anyone else less; I just have more room to love.

I was standing in line in the grocery store when a stranger looked at the diapers and cereal in my cart and said, "I could have been a great mother if I hadn't had one of my own." I laughed, thinking it was a joke, but her face didn't move a muscle. Not one of us had a "perfect mother." None of us will be a perfect mother. But God's love is perfect and pure. Whether you are a mother or not, ask God to quicken your heart to what his Word says: "Can a mother forget the baby at her breast and have no compassion on the child she has borne? Though she may forget, I will not forget you! See, I have engraved you on the palms of my hands; your walls are ever before me" (Isaiah 49:15–16).

God declares, "I carried you on eagles' wings and brought you to myself" (Exodus 19:4). (It's the mother eagle who carries the young!) And Jesus himself said to the city of Jerusalem, "How often I have longed to gather your children together, as a hen gathers her chicks under her wings, but you were not willing" (Matthew 23:37).

The story is told of a terrible fire on a farm that wiped out everything the farmer owned. When the flames had died down the farmer walked sadly through the smoldering mass of all that was left of his life's work. His boot caught the charred body of a hen. When he turned it over, he discovered tiny, peeping chicks, alive and well under the body of their mother. She had given her life to protect her young. To me a mother's love is a God-given gift, a glimpse of heaven, a picture seen through smoky glass of how passionately God's heart beats for us.

Julian of Norwich compared God's love to a mother's love: "The earthly mother lovingly understands her child and sees its every need; she keeps it most tenderly, for such is the true nature and condition of motherhood. Then as it grows older, her working changes, but never her love. For when it is older still, she allows it to be chastised so as to break down its vices and so help the child receive virtues and graces." She continues, "This same work"—of loving, comforting, disciplining—"our Lord himself does."

Lest you think I'm discounting the father love of God, consider one verse buried in the Old Testament story of King

David. His son—his rebel son who was leading a coup against David—was killed. David's response: "My son, my son Absalom! If only I had died instead of you—O Absalom, my son, my son!" (2 Samuel 18:33).

Do you see it? God did die for you. He did it for love.

What a gift! It is beyond human comprehension to fathom the depth of this love. God the Son dying for me. But, you say, how could God the Father send God the Son to die? How could a father do that to a son? I think maybe we don't fully understand the unity of the love and purpose of the Trinity. In ways we don't understand the Father and Son and Holy Spirit are one—the I AM. John 1:1 says, "The Word was with God, and the Word was God." And in John 10:18 Jesus says he lays down his life "of my own accord. I have authority to lay it down and authority to take it up again. This command I received from my Father."

Check out John 3:16–18. "God so loved the world that he gave his one and only Son, that whoever believes in him shall not perish but have eternal life. For God did not send his Son into the world to condemn the world, but to save the world through him. Whoever believes in him is not condemned." In the first rush of salvation, we claim that salvation from condemnation. And from then on we may live with the assurance that we are saved from eternal condemnation, but too many of us hold onto the daily feelings of condemnation—not really laying claim to the work of Christ on the cross. The abundant life he promises for here and now. We don't believe that God is love. We choose to believe that God is angry.

God Is Faithful

In Greek the word for *faith* is the same as the word for *faithful*. We place our faith in a God who is faithful—even if and when we don't "get the plan."

Let me give you an illustration from my own life with baby Christian. Christian does not like his car seat. I wasn't prepared for this. My nephew, David, was comforted by his car seat more than anything else, and I thought all babies came that way. Apparently not. Some days Christian can be distracted by his plastic frog or by his biter bunny or by Barry and me singing "Jesus loves me, this I know" at the top of our lungs, but there are days when nothing helps and he wails like someone being tortured. He just doesn't get it. He wants to be held. I watched him in the rearview mirror the other day, and all of a sudden I saw myself in him. He was red faced and cross. I couldn't explain to a six-month-old baby that the reason he was in a car seat was for his own good. I couldn't make him understand that it was *because* I loved him that he was strapped in to this contraption. All he knew was that he wanted out, that his mother had the power to do it, and that she wouldn't.

I saw how I must seem to God so many times. I don't always understand what the Lord is doing in and through my life. I must seem to God to be a red-faced screaming little baby who thinks she knows best and actually doesn't have a clue. And yet as I watch him turn all the colors of the rainbow, I love him passionately. Just as I will never stop the car and toss Christian out, God in his faithfulness holds on to us when we "don't like the plan." "The Lord is faithful, and he will strengthen and protect you" (2 Thessalonians 3:3).

The Bible uses another image as an example of God's faithfulness to us: God the loving, faithful spouse. Imagine, for a moment, this conversation between a father and a son about the son's future bride.

"She's the one for you, son. I'm sure of it."

Martin looked at his father in utter disbelief. "You must be joking!" he said. "She's hardly the kind of woman you should be advising me to marry."

"I'm as serious as I've ever been," his father continued. "I'm telling you, this is the girl you should marry."

Martin looked across the restaurant to the bar where his "intended" was creating quite a stir. She was on her fourth round of drinks and was getting louder with every clink of glasses. He watched as four of the guys at the bar threw their car keys into a beer glass and held it up for Sonja to choose. She pulled out a set of keys that went with the blue suit and disappeared into the night.

"I'm asking you to do this for me, son," his father said. "Do this for me."

An episode from a cheap soap opera? Just read the Old Testament book of Hosea. This man of God was instructed to marry a woman "with a reputation" to live out the story of God's faithfulness to unfaithful Israel. Hosea married Gomer, who remained unfaithful to him, and yet Hosea persisted in his faithfulness. Perhaps God, in the only way we can understand, is giving us an illustration of how we have broken his heart by our wanderings, our lack of love and commitment. What is so amazing about the tragic story of Hosea and Gomer is the redemption and mercy carved out on the harsh landscape of their lives. We read, "The LORD said to me, 'Go, show your love to your wife again, though she is loved by another and is an adulteress. Love her as the LORD loves the Israelites, though they turn to other gods" (Hosea 3:1). Despite the brazen behavior of his people, God still loves, still goes after, still stands true and faithful.

My life philosophy in a nutshell is "Life is tough but God is faithful."

Faithful to what? you might ask. He is faithful not to tempt us beyond what we can bear (1 Corinthians 10:13). If we confess our sins, he will faithfully forgive them (1 John 1:9). And finally, even if we are faithless, he promises to remain faithful (2 Timothy 2:13).

Have you ever seen the old black-and-white movie of Robert Louis Stevenson's *Kidnapped?* There is a terrifying scene: The wicked uncle sends young David to climb the steps to the top of an old tower. It's very dark, and David can hardly see one step in front of another. Suddenly lightning streaks across the sky—just as David is about to step off the last step and tumble to his death. The first time I saw it I almost jumped out of my skin—realizing David had been *set up.*

That's the opposite of how our God works. He never ever sets us up to fall.

Another Scripture says this about God's faithfulness: "May your whole spirit, soul and body be kept blameless at the coming of our Lord Jesus Christ. The one who calls you is faithful and he will do it" (1 Thessalonians 5:23–24). There is a great mystery at work here. We are called, but God will do it. Does that mean that we relax in our La-Z-Boy for the soul? Not at all. We are called to run the race, and yet the coach has promised that he will make sure we finish. Do you ever feel like throwing in the towel? Do you ever despair when it seems the finish line is a long way off and you're tired out already? There is joy and comfort and courage to be found in this promise: "Being confident of this, that he who began a good work in you will carry it on to completion until the day of Christ Jesus" (Philippians 1:6).

God Is the God of Hope

In one sense the entire Bible shines as a witness that our God is the God of hope, as described in Romans 15:13 (and in relationship to joy!): "May the God of hope fill you with all joy and peace as you trust in him, so that you may overflow with hope by the power of the Holy Spirit." Paul called himself an apostle of "Christ Jesus our hope" (1 Timothy 1:1).

The dictionary defines *hope* as, "To wish for something with expectation of its fulfillment. To have confidence; trust." I think we have degraded the word *hope* and stripped it of its deepest meaning. We "hope" for good weather for a picnic. We "hope" that our politicians live up to their promises. But most of the time we think it'll probably rain and expect that our leaders' words will dissolve like ice cubes on a summer's day. Hope in God, a faithful, loving God, is not like that. It's not like anything else on earth. Banks fail, leaders fail, churches fail, but God never fails.

And as the faithful God of hope looks at us, even in our faithless wanderings, he hopes in us. Think of the picture of the father who waits every day for the prodigal son. We tune in on the day of the homecoming—but he has been there every day. Who knows how long that has been, as months turn into years without as much as a phone call and yet he waits, yet he hopes. What love! Always hopeful for reconciliation, for deeper communion, for heart intimacy with his child. Always hopeful even for the "older brother" to be all he is because "you are always with me and everything I have is yours." We look for "good guys" and "bad guys" in stories. In this story of our relationship with God, we are all the "bad guys" made the "good guys" through Christ.

Jesus said, "I am ... the truth" (John 14:6). He said, "The truth will set you free" (John 8:32)—free to live life "to the full" (John 10:10), which is what joy is all about.

JESSICA'S STORY

We became friends when I was nineteen. I was a student in London and she was the mother of one of my fellow students. As they lived in London and I was miles away from my Scottish home, the family took me under their wings. I spent many weekends with them and grew to love them all. On one particular occasion I woke up early and wandered down to the kitchen to make some coffee and caught Jessica sitting at the breakfast table with tears pouring down her face. I was embarrassed. I stood still for a moment, wondering if I should say anything or tiptoe back upstairs, when she looked up and saw me.

"I'm sorry," I said. "I didn't know you were up."

"Sit down, Sheila," she said, wiping her eyes with the corner of her dressing gown.

"Can I get you anything?" I asked.

"No, I'm fine!" she said, and then laughed wryly. "Well, I guess it's obvious that I'm not fine."

For some reason she decided to talk to me. Perhaps she had no one else, or there was comfort in knowing that I would leave that day and head back to school.

"I can't believe that Paul and I have been so foolish," she began.

I wondered what she was going to tell me as she brought her husband into the story.

"When we met we were so in love. He was the most wonderful man I had ever met. It had been my dream to meet a man who loved God and would love me with all his heart." She stopped for a moment and I felt like an intruder. "We married a year later, and even though our house was small we loved it. It was a home and a haven for us. The young people from our church would crowd into our den for Bible studies, and they would leave with the aroma of pizza and a parable in the air. We knew that we had something special. Then the children came along." She smiled at a picture on the refrigerator door of the three children when they were young piled on top of each other on a beach. "We threw ourselves into raising them. They became our life. This year the final one will graduate from college, and I don't know Paul anymore. We've become strangers apart from the children. I'm dreading us being alone, because I don't know what we'll talk about." She laid her head on the kitchen table and wept. I moved beside her and put my arm around her and said nothing. What could I say? I felt so sad.

I've never forgotten Jessica. We didn't stay in touch, but her life bumped mine enough to mark it for life.

The older I get the more I realize what she was saying to me about relationships—especially my relationship with God. God and I aren't strangers living under the same roof. We are abiding in and with each other. Of course communication and intimacy with God isn't quite as easy to identify as it is with a human companion. But we do have one definite place to look for God—his Word.

FESTOON YOURSELF WITH THE WORD

How do we get to know this God who is love, who is faithful, who is the God of hope?

We can start by what C. S. Lewis called "festooning in the Word of God." *Festooning* is an old-fashioned word that refers to stringing up a garland of flowers. Lewis calls us to cover ourselves with the words of God.

Drape your soul with garlands of God's Word. Isn't that a wonderful picture! I can't think of a more festive covering to be seen in or to delight in.

As you open your Bible I suggest you pray a very specific prayer—that the Holy Spirit will highlight for you truths that you need to "hear" about who he is. If you don't feel the love of God deep within your being, look for it in his Word. Read the Song of Songs—allow yourself to see God as your perfect, loving spouse. Read the book of Ruth—allow yourself to see Godlike qualities in the figure of Boaz—covering and protecting and redeeming Ruth, though she was a foreigner in a new land. Read the gospel of John, the book of Romans. This is not a prescription; it's a gift list.

I remember the very first card that Barry ever sent to me. I read it over and over for hours, making sure that I had squeezed every nuance and thought from the words on the page. I still have it. God has written the most radical love letter of all, so drape yourself with it. Wear it everywhere you go. It was written to you to fill you with joy.

Marcus Aurelius, the second-century Roman emperor, said that "the most important thing a man can choose is what he thinks." We allow old negative tapes to play in our head. Lies of the enemy torment us and cause us to believe that we will never finish our race. We need to replace those worn-out tapes with truth, with the Word of God.

Jude 21 admonishes Christians to "keep yourselves in God's love as you wait for the mercy of our Lord Jesus Christ to bring you to eternal life." We have a choice in how we think. Romans 12:2 says we are to "be transformed by the renewing of your mind" so that we are "able to test and approve what God's will is—his good, pleasing and perfect will."

I have dealt with fear all of my life. In the last few years I have begun to step out from under that load, but when I feel it stirring in me again, I drown it in the Word of God.

> *The LORD is my light and my salvation—whom shall I fear? The LORD is the stronghold of my life—of whom shall I be afraid? When evil men advance against me to devour my flesh, when my enemies and my foes attack me, they will stumble and fall. Though an army besiege me, my heart will not fear; though war break out against me, even then will I be confident. One thing I ask of the LORD, this is what I seek: that I may dwell in the house of the LORD all the days of my life, to gaze upon the beauty of the LORD and to seek him in his temple. For in the day of trouble he will keep me safe in his dwelling; he will hide me in the shelter of his tabernacle and set me high upon a rock.*
>
> Psalm 27:1–5

I have committed part of this psalm to heart, and I repeat it out loud, and even as I hear my voice, I feel hope and faith rising up inside me.

When I was breast-feeding Christian, I would pray for him and cherish these verses:

> *Yet you brought me out of the womb; you made me trust in you even at my mother's breast. From birth I was cast upon you; from my mother's womb you have been my God.*
>
> Psalm 22:9–10

As you start to read the Word, rebuke the father of lies. A friend of mine recently had a dramatic turn in her relationship with God. As she drew close to him and asked him to show her his true self, she started to see "light" and love in the Scriptures. She is convinced that her own negative responses—her own shame and self-loathing as a result of the lies she was believing—were "highlighting" the negatives in Scripture. As you read God's Word, trust the God who is faithful to show you the way through truth to the abundant life of joy.

In his book *Praying the Scriptures,* Judson Cornwall tells the story of a young man he counseled—a man he described as "flitting around like a kite with too short a tail." Cornwall asked him about his Bible-reading habits. The man answered, "I really don't have time to read the Bible. I am a student at the university, and my studies consume my reading time. I give myself to prayer. I leave it to others to read the Bible."

Cornwall answered with some specific advice, "May I earnestly urge you to divide your prayer time between devotionally reading the Bible and emotionally calling upon God? You need to know better the God to whom you are praying, and you need to hear the Lord speak to you through his Word. You are conducting a monologue and calling it prayer."

Do you ever do that yourself? Relationship with God calls for two-way conversation. Let yourself listen; let yourself be nourished.

FRUIT OF THE TRUE VINE

As I write these words I think of a pastor's wife who is afraid to get help with her depression. I think of those who have written to me and said, "I want to know this joy that you talk about, but life is so hard." I think of another young woman whose parting words to me at a church were, "Now I'll go and work on joy." Joy is not a new burden to pick up and drag around. You can't go out and work on joy. We are called to rest in the One who *is* joy.

I remember on a trip through France seeing grapes fall off the vines because the fruit was so heavy and ready to be harvested. The thought of the vine *trying* to produce grapes is ridiculous. To paraphrase a bumper sticker slogan: Grapes happen! Grapes happen when there are good roots, water, and pruning—then fruit is a given. Remember the promise of John 15:4? "Remain in me, and I will remain in you. No branch can bear fruit by itself; it must remain in the vine. Neither can you bear fruit unless you remain in me." So we are called to rest in Christ because without him there is no fruit, no joy.

When our newborn son was in the hospital and we didn't know what was wrong, I struggled with panic and fear that was based on a distortion of who God is. In my despair as a new mom with a sick baby, I had pasted onto God an image of a god who randomly puts his subjects through tests as if on a power trip. At one point I slipped away, down the hall, into the room reserved for mothers to pump their breast milk. I put up the *reserved* sign and got down on my knees.

"Lord, I want to trust you here. I want to lean on you and say, 'Whatever, Lord'—not my will but yours—but I'm so afraid to, in case you take him, and I don't think that I could bear that. Please help me!"

I stayed there for a long, long time, and I suddenly remembered that God had been there before me. He had watched his boy kneeling in a garden, blood flowing down his face. More than that, I remembered who he is. He is my faithful Father who loves me, who loves Barry, and who loves our little boy. I knelt down broken and afraid, and when I left that room I was still afraid, but I was leaning on the Lord.

I'm very grateful for the freedom to be honest with God. I celebrate that. I believe that we do our relationship a disservice when we cover up the raw, broken parts of our lives. I used to think that if I loved God enough, he would keep all the bad things outside my door, but I know that's not true anymore. My baby might have died. Many mothers have faced that horrible loss. But they have not been alone. The faithful, loving God is with them.

I stopped outside of Christian's room and listened as his daddy sang to him,

> *Jesus loves me this I know*
> *For the Bible tells me so*
> *Little ones to him belong*
> *They are weak but he is strong.*

I joined in.

> *Yes, Jesus loves me*
> *Yes, Jesus loves me*
> *Yes, Jesus loves me*
> *The Bible tells me so.*

GETTING TO JOY

1. Go to a good friend (or family member) and ask this person to remind you of two ways that God has been faithful to you in the last five years. Sometimes others can see graces that we are blind to.

2. Mentally review any "Disappointments with God" that you wrote down (and buried) after reading chapter 2. Bring any that you specifically remember to God and ask him to give you new insight regarding them in light of his love, faithfulness, and hope for you and your maturity. Write a new list of ways that God has been faithful.

3. Write out a one- or two-sentence statement of who you know God to be. Stick it on your refrigerator door for a while. Every time you pass by, read it aloud. Allow truth to become as etched in your heart and mind as any previous misunderstandings about God have been.

4. Buy a Scripture verse-a-day calendar and place it where you will see it often. Turn the day's verse over and over in your mind and let it soak into your heart. Meditate on it. Memorize it. Make up a tune and sing it—to help you festoon yourself with God's Word.

CHAPTER 6

JOY: CLOTHING YOU WERE MEANT TO WEAR

When I consider your heavens, the work of your fingers, the moon and the stars, which you have set in place, what is man that you are mindful of him, the son of man that you care for him?

Psalm 8:3–4

W e've talked about the truth about God—the I AM, who was and is and will be. But God is only half of this relationship. What does God's Word say about you and me—who we were, who we are, and who we will be?

THE TRUE CHRISTIAN

What does a true Christian look like? As a child I pictured the true Christian as being a missionary. (I was sure that was what lay ahead for me.) Here's what she looked like: Bangs cut extra short out of good stewardship so that she wouldn't need another haircut for at least six months. The rest of her hair pulled so tightly in a bun that she looked permanently surprised. (There would be no room for impure thoughts as they were all strangled to death.) Brown skirt down to just above her ankles so she would not cause anyone to stumble. On top she wore a knitted sweater buttoned up to her chin. No makeup. No jewelry.

A true Christian?
Maybe not!

WE ARE MADE IN GOD'S IMAGE

In the first chapter of the Bible, man and woman make a glorious entrance. "Then God said, 'Let us make man in our image, in our likeness, and let them rule over the fish of the sea and the birds of the air.'. . . So God created man in his own image, in the image of God he created him; male and female he created them. God blessed them" (Genesis 1:26 28). Made in the image of God! What does that look like? We are made to be loving, faithful, true, compassionate, kind, creative, righteous, strong, tender, eternal. All the things we long for are things we were made for. It is interesting to note how we as a society are moving away from God in search of what can be found only in him. We look for meaning and purpose, for hope and fulfillment in the ash trays of the world. Adam and Eve bathed daily in what we thirst for. Imagine with me if you will.

Morning. The sun gently kisses them awake. Another perfect day. The garden is rich in every pure blossom imaginable. The scent is intoxicating. The best of foods are laid before them, and all they desire brings health and strength to their beautiful bodies. Crystal waters wash over them as they bathe together, naked, unashamed, strong, and glorious. The animals watch from every bush and tree in awe of Adam and Eve, the ones God talks to. Every evening as the sun wishes them good night, the Creator of the garden walks with them, his presence pouring life into their souls, his words weaving unspeakably beautiful tapestries in their hearts. They are known, face to face. There are no secrets, no shame, no sorrow or tears. There is no loneliness but moments of solitude so rich it is almost unbearable. There is joy, pure joy, in the garden.

Does it ever overwhelm you that God would love his human creation so much? I think it was almost more than David could bear at times. "When I consider your heavens, the work of your fingers, the moon and the stars, which you have set in place, what is man that you are mindful of him, the son of man that you care for him? You made him a little lower than the heavenly beings and crowned him with glory and honor" (Psalm 8:3–5). We live in a world that stands in awe of very little. But stop for a moment and reflect. The God of the universe has chosen you to know him! It's like crawling out of a ditch covered in mud and debris and being put on the best-dressed list. It's like being handed the Pulitzer Prize for literature when you can barely write your own name. It's like showing up with empty pockets at a benefit dinner for the needy and being voted benefactor of the year.

One thing is clear. At creation we were dressed in the finest apparel—purity before God and one another. We were draped in the most glorious cloth of all—intimate fellowship with God.

WE ARE SINNERS FALLEN FROM INNOCENCE

But life in the Garden is not life as we know it. Something happened. You no doubt know the Genesis account. Adam and Eve had everything. Everything except the opportunity to say no. And that was what they grasped for. That was what they gave everything away for—free will. It wasn't enough to be "a little less than." They allowed themselves to entertain the idea, "perhaps we can be more than."

John Milton in *Paradise Lost* proposes this scenario leading up to the fateful fall in Eden: that Satan and other fallen angels gathered together at a council hall, appropriately named Pandemonium, to discuss how to wound God. It's decided that the most effective way would be to corrupt God's new creation, man. Satan flew out of hell and tricked an angel into telling him where to find Eden. He worked his wiles on Eve. She ate the forbidden fruit. And Adam—for love of Eve—also bit into the fruit.

In that scene everything changed.

Suddenly they were arguing bitterly and accusing each other. Adam blamed Eve. Eve blamed the serpent. It's the first human war.

Suddenly they were trying to cover themselves with fig leaves, because they "saw" their guilt, which was evidenced as the shame of their nakedness or humanity.

Suddenly they were estranged from God, hiding from him behind the bushes.

Suddenly life was hard—there was pain, there was domination and intimidation, there were thorns and thistles, there was back-breaking work, there was physical death: "Dust you are and to dust you will return" (Genesis 3:19).

And suddenly they and all their descendants to this day have been subject to spiritual death, as described in Romans 5:12: "Sin entered the world through one man, and death through sin, and in this way death came to all men, because all sinned."

In Romans 3:23 Paul says it even more clearly: "All have sinned and fall short of the glory of God." As Neal Lozano says in *The Older Brother Returns*, "We will never grasp the significance of sin unless we realize the significance of falling short of the glory of God." Can you imagine the offense to God? To offer created beings everything. To offer relationship with God, the unknowable. To shower a man and a woman with every good gift asking only one thing in return, one sign of love and loyalty.

I find it hard to believe that there is one more day of human history after the Eden rebellion. If I were God, that day would have been the last on planet Earth. He owed us nothing. He gave us everything, and yet we flew in his face and said no! Did all of heaven reverberate with the cry of anguish from God's heart as Eve bit into the fruit?

I take a bit of comfort in my reading of the fall of Adam and Eve. If, as Milton proposed, Satan set out to find a way to "wound God," he hit it. The God I see in Geneses 3 was wounded and grieved by Adam and Eve's choice—their disobedience and sin—more than angry at them. He cursed the serpent. He cursed the ground because of Adam. But the word *curse* isn't directed toward Adam and Eve. Yes, they would know incredible hardship and grief, they would know death, they would be banished from the garden of delight. But he did not seem to speak to them in anger. And as for their new awareness of their unworthiness and shame? Genesis 3:21 indicates the Lord took some pity. (Maybe he saw the absurdity of their fig-leaf aprons.) "The LORD God made garments of skin for Adam and his wife and clothed them." That telling sentence describes the act of a God who loves the man and woman— made in his image—broken and soiled though they be.

I have an image strong in my mind as I write these words. When I was sixteen I was a volunteer at a geriatric hospital. I was a shy teenager, uncomfortable with my blossoming sexuality and the differences between men and women. One evening as I was taking cups of cocoa to the patients, an old man without his pajama bottoms stepped out of the bathroom. He was obviously distressed. He had soiled them and left them on the floor and now stood partially naked before a sixteen-year-old girl. In that moment my heart was filled with compassion for this man who could have been my grandfather. I quickly grabbed a blanket from the laundry cupboard and wrapped it around him and showed him back to his bed. He seemed so grateful. I think this is what God did for Adam and Eve. They stood naked, exposed, and God wrapped a blanket around them—as Christ robes us who believe in him with his robes of righteousness.

Speaking of the Fall and the shame of Adam and Eve, Melvin Hugen and Cornelius Plantinga ("Naked and Exposed," *Books and Culture*, March-April 1996) say, "Human beings generate shame; God covers it with a durable product that requires the shedding of blood. Human beings suffer a metaphysical chill; God warms them with garments they should never have needed."

WE ARE ROBED IN JESUS' RIGHTEOUSNESS

In the Old Testament a goat would be brought forward and the sins of the people would symbolically be laid upon him. This scapegoat would be led out into the wilderness to a place so remote that he would never find his way back. But it was temporary. This process had to be repeated every year.

But then something happened. God himself—holy, perfect, spotless—stepped in to take that sin upon himself. "When we were still powerless, Christ died for the ungodly.... God demonstrates his own love for us in this: While we were still sinners, Christ died for us" (Romans 5:6, 8).

And in 2 Corinthians 5:21 Paul says, "God made him who had no sin to be sin for us, so that in him we might become the righteousness of God." I wish I had Oswald Chambers's ability to explain spiritual truths. I don't, so read closely his explanation of this verse, as recorded in *My Utmost for His Highest*:

> Sin is a fundamental relationship; it is not wrong doing, it is wrong *being*, deliberate and emphatic independence of God. The Christian religion bases everything on the positive, radical nature of sin. Other religions deal with sins; the Bible alone deals with sin. The first thing Jesus Christ faced in men was the heredity of sin, and it is because we have ignored this in our presentation of the Gospel that the message of the Gospel has lost its sting and its blasting power.
>
> The revelation of the Bible is not that Jesus Christ took upon himself our fleshly sins, but that he took upon himself the heredity of sin which no man can touch. God made his own Son to be sin that he might make the sinner a saint.... He deliberately took upon his own shoulders and bore in his own Person, the whole massed sin of the human race.... He put [the human race] back to where God designed it to be, and anyone can enter into union with God on the grounds of what our Lord has done on the cross.

I am writing this book primarily for Christian women—who have a basic understanding of Christ coming to earth, dying, rising from the dead. But do we really understand what he did for us? He has made us right with God—a rightness based on Christ's righteousness, not on ours. There's nothing we can do to earn this rightness.

Isaiah uses a strong image to describe our attempts to redeem ourselves or to impress God: "All our righteous acts are like filthy rags" (64:6). He's talking about menstrual rags—fit for the garbage heap.

As Neal Lozano says: "Our good works, our long prayers, our years of service, can never earn us one drop of our Savior's blood. We will never deserve God's love; and yet, wretches that we are, he pours his love upon us as a gift. It is a gift we must choose to receive—with humility, reverence, and awe, always aware that we, though made worthy, are unworthy." It is a gift we choose to receive once—at that hour when we first believe. We choose to receive it at our baptism. And then we must continue to receive it every day, as if it were a new set of clothes, replacing those fig leaves we try to hide behind.

In dying Christ covered us, clothed us, with his righteousness. Looking forward to the Messiah, the prophet Isaiah says, "Instead of their shame my people will receive a double portion ... and everlasting joy will be theirs.... My soul rejoices in my God. For he has clothed me with garments of salvation and arrayed me in a robe of righteousness ... as a bride adorns herself with her jewels" (61:7, 10).

There is something so fresh and joyful about that image. It captures the thought of all the time that a bride invests in that day above all other days. Nothing is too good, because only the best will do.

Christ clothes us, yes, but Galatians 3:27 also says that we have clothed ourselves with Christ. "You are all sons of God through faith in Christ Jesus, for all of you who were baptized into Christ have clothed yourselves with Christ." In his book *Riding the Wind*, Terry Fullam explains the original, secular meaning of the Greek word for *baptize*. "When a piece of unbleached muslin was plunged into a huge vat of bright red dye, it was baptized—saturated, covered over, put under—so that it totally took on the new color. Not one corner would be left untouched and uncovered." Christ has clothed us— covered us—with his righteousness, and we are to clothe ourselves with him.

At this point in my life the most difficult task that I attempt in any given day is to get clothes on my son. He wriggles. He moves at the wrong moment. I'll get one leg in his suit, and he'll crawl off after a toy or a fly, and I'm back to square one. Every now and then he'll lie back and bless his mother with the opportunity to clothe him without requiring oxygen at the end of it, and I count my blessings. So too we are called to relax in God and allow him to clothe us in his righteousness.

Ephesians 2:8–9 says, "For it is by grace you have been saved, through faith—and this not from yourselves, it is the gift of God—not by works, so that no one can boast."

That's what's so amazing about grace! We are loved. We are saved by faith. We don't have to prove ourselves to God. We simply have to believe in the power of his redemptive work and receive it as our own.

At this point you may be asking a question the apostle Paul posed to his first-century readers. *If God loves me just the way I am, why shouldn't I continue to wallow in the muck?* "What shall we say, then? Shall we go on sinning so that grace may increase?" (Romans 6:1).

Paul answered his own question: "By no means!" In Christ we are new creatures. With Christ we "died to sin" (v. 2), so why would we want to live in it any longer? If we intentionally set out to test the limits of God's grace, we haven't understood it. We haven't grasped the truth of the gospel, which draws us and calls us to be like Christ himself.

The New Testament Greek word for *grace*—the gift of God—is *charis*. And the Greek word for joy is *chara*. They both have the same root. And I propose that as our heads and hearts learn the truth about the grace of our Lord, we become able to wear the joy of our Lord. Wear the joy? Yes—that's the image used in the prayer of Psalm 30:11–12: "You removed my sackcloth and clothed me with joy, that my heart may sing to you and not be silent."

Joy may be fruit we were meant to bear. It is also clothing we are meant to wear—as we live in the truth of who we are in Christ: sinners saved by grace, living under the mercy of a loving God, empowered by the Spirit of the living God.

WE ARE CHILDREN GROWING IN GOD'S SPIRIT

When Jesus left this earth, he promised to send the Holy Spirit, the Comforter, the Empowerer. We are not left alone on this journey. We couldn't make this journey alone. As Martin Luther said, "If we in our own strength confide, our striving would be losing." Not only do we have a companion, but we also have joy in all circumstances of life, because God's love is poured into our hearts through the Holy Spirit.

> *We rejoice in the hope of the glory of God. Not only so, but we also rejoice in our sufferings, because we know that suffering produces perseverance; perseverance, character; and character, hope. And hope does not disappoint us, because God has poured out his love into our hearts by the Holy Spirit, whom he has given us.*
>
> Romans 5:2–5

Joy is a garment we were created to wear. It is a custom fit. It is a gift to us as we daily bring our lives to God and ask to be filled again. "May the God of hope fill you with all joy and peace as you trust in him, so that you may overflow with hope by the power of the Holy Spirit" (Romans 15:13).

In the next chapter, we'll look at the joy of walking in the truth, which leads us to freedom. It is the Spirit who leads us on this journey toward joy, peace, hope, and truth. "But when he, the Spirit of truth, comes, he will guide you into all truth. He will not speak on his own; he will speak only what he hears, and he will tell you what is yet to come" (John 16:13). It's a mystery to me—this collaboration between the triune God and his children. But one thing I do know is this: When there is no joy in my life, it's because I have stopped resting in Christ; I'm trying to do it all by myself again. I can choose to wear myself into the ground trying to produce something impressive in my life, or I can rest safe in the arms of Jesus, and the "fruit of the Spirit" of Christ is a given. Joy is there.

WE ARE SAINTS AWAITING
OUR GLORIFICATION

Are we living in the Garden of Eden? No. The park was closed. Or in the heavenly city—"in the land where we'll never grow old"? No. Not yet.

Here and now, redeemed though we are, life is hard. Our redemption has been bought, but even so, "We know that the whole creation has been groaning as in the pains of childbirth right up to the present time. Not only so, but we ourselves, who have the firstfruits of the Spirit, groan inwardly as we wait eagerly for our adoption as sons, the redemption of our bodies.... If we hope for what we do not yet have, we wait for it patiently" (Romans 8:22–25).

And yet, here and now, this side of our final glorification, we are called to be saints. Note the line of Oswald Chambers's: "God made his own Son to be sin that he might make the sinner a saint." Me? A saint? By virtue of Christ's redemption, yes. Nearly all of Paul's epistles—even those that prod Christians toward a more holy life—are addressed to "the saints" or "those called to be saints." Those called to be holy.

But, you may say (along with me), I trip and stumble and fall short of the glory of God—still, even though I "believe," even though my heart wants to please God.

Even here we are not alone. The very next words of Romans 8 read: "In the same way, the Spirit helps us in our weakness.... The Spirit intercedes for the saints in accordance with God's will" (vv. 26–27). And Paul's message keeps going: "And we know that in all things God works for the good of those who love him, who have been called according to his purpose" (v. 28).

In the fall of '97 I was a guest speaker along with Max Lucado on a cruise to Bermuda. One night stands out for me. We were docked in the port of St. George on the island of Bermuda and had been given permission to hold a communion service at St. Peter's Church that evening. The church was built in the seventeenth century and has held services continually since that time. About a hundred of us gathered together in this beautiful old building to celebrate the Lord's Supper. The church was illuminated by candles, and as we sang together I felt that our voices were blending in a hymn of praise with all who had gone before us.

Max spoke. He reminded us that Christ laid down his crown to come to this earth and live among us. He laid it down and only took it up again once and that was to place it on your head. When he, the innocent lamb of God, took our sin on himself, we through faith in him took on his righteousness. He took the crown off his head and placed it on yours, placed it on mine. Who can understand such a gift? We come to God with nothing and we are given everything. There is nothing you can do to earn it, to be worthy of this love. It is a gift. And if you did nothing to earn it, there is nothing you can do to lose it apart from walking away from the Gift Giver.

On the evening designated for formal attire on the cruise, I watched the crowd pour into the dining room. Some wore glorious creations that must have cost a fortune. Some came draped in sequins and pearls. Men twisted uncomfortably in tuxedos that looked a little too small or too stiff. I smiled and enjoyed the event—people dressed appropriately for the occasion. But for a moment later that evening I paused and reflected on the eternal truth about clothing: Someday when we all come together before the throne of grace, we will be dressed in only one thing, the robes of righteousness purchased for us by Christ.

Clothe me, clothe me with yourself, eternal truth.

Catherine of Siena

GETTING TO JOY

1. Take a look at your wardrobe. What colors are most predominant? I went through a stage when almost all my clothes were black, a somber reflection of my mood. I began to add in some other colors that made me feel good to wear.

Take a trip to the mall. Buy yourself one new outfit in your favorite color. Every time you wear it, remind yourself that you are clothed in the beauty of Christ.

2. Take a walk today. Notice the flowers and trees, the birds and butterflies. Or go to a florist's shop or browse through a fruit stand. Remind yourself that the God who clothes the flowers of the field clothes you (see Matthew 6:28–30).

3. Buy or pick a small bouquet. Note how effortlessly nature bears her fruit and wears her colorful clothing. Give your flowers away to someone you meet today who looks as if she is weighed down with the pain and sin of the whole world. With your gift give a very brief explanation, such as "This is for you. God loves you." Or, "Here, God wants to brighten your day."

4. Each day this week as you put on your makeup, ask God to clothe you spiritually for the day ahead. Ask him to clothe you with joy.

5. Choose to meditate on these Scriptures:

God made him who had no sin to be sin for us, so that in him we might become the righteousness of God.
2 Corinthians 5:21

Instead of their shame my people will receive a double portion . . . and everlasting joy will be theirs. . . . My soul rejoices in my God. For he has clothed me with garments of salvation and arrayed me in a robe of righteousness . . . as a bride adorns herself with her jewels.
Isaiah 61:7, 10

You are all sons of God through faith in Christ Jesus, for all of you who were baptized into Christ have clothed yourselves with Christ.
Galatians 3:26–27

You removed my sackcloth and clothed me with joy, that my heart may sing to you and not be silent.
Psalm 30:11–12

CHAPTER 7

THE JOY OF WALKING IN THE TRUTH

I have no greater joy than to hear that my children are walking in the truth.

3 John 4

The problem with most people is not in finding the truth but in facing it.

Anonymous

ﮮ

We've looked at some truths about God and some truths about ourselves. What do these mean for us Christian women? The women I meet who want to please him? Who are exhausted in their efforts to serve him? Who want to know the strength that is the joy of the Lord? What is the connection between the joy of the Lord and walking in the truth?

Jesus himself said that it was possible for believers to "know the truth, and the truth will set you free" (John 8:32).

How can we get there? The journey to joy starts as we turn our attention to the great I AM and off ourselves.

In the 1950s Dag Hammarskjöld moved from his native Sweden to New York, where he was secretary-general of the United Nations. After his tragic death, journal-like reflections, titled *Markings*, were published that revealed him as a deeply spiritual man. He reasoned that self-centeredness destroys human life; it's only when we lose ourselves in God that we find a sense of purpose.

Of course there's nothing new about self-centeredness. It's been the problem from the beginning. Lucifer was not content to be who he was, to accept his createdness and worship the Creator. Adam and Eve traded the perfect peace of the Garden and the deepest, intimate fellowship with God to grasp for a chance to be like him.

Sometimes we in the church think it is only those "out there" who are self-absorbed—the yuppies who need a good dose of teaching about the need for self-control and sharing. But I think as "good, responsible Christians," our own joy is often blocked because of our preoccupation with ourselves. Virtually all of the saboteurs to joy can be tracked back to one root. They assume that "I" am center stage. I smiled when I found out that the word *idiot* comes from the Greek root *idios*, which means "self." Too often we Christians are like the man described by George Eliot: "He was like a cock, who thought the sun had risen to hear him crow."

Our efforts are very often well intentioned. Can you identify with the effort of trying to be a hero for Jesus? I used to walk the beach at night after our youth group meetings and steel myself to be a Navy Seal for Christ. But we've got the wrong idea. Our life of faith—and faithfulness—starts and ends with God, not with ourselves.

Think in terms of this parable: The owner of an antique shop put a price tag of four million dollars on a cheap, cracked pot and set it on a shelf. No one could understand the exorbitant price. It was obviously a fairly worthless piece. But the vase began to change. Rather than being humbled and grateful to be put on a "worthy" shelf, the chipped vase began to look down on the other vases as she observed her own price tag. The truth was that in and of herself she was still a cheap, chipped vase, but the owner had placed worth on her. There would be no point in the vase sending out brochures promoting herself because it would be ridiculous; she would be laughed

at. Her only value rested in the one who owned her and gave
her his value.

A joyful journey in truth starts here:

> *Let us throw off everything that hinders and the sin that so easily
> entangles, and let us run with perseverance the race marked out for
> us.* Let us fix our eyes on Jesus, the author and perfecter [fin-
> isher] of our faith, *who for the joy set before him endured the cross,
> scorning its shame, and sat down at the right hand of the throne
> of God. Consider him who endured such opposition from sinful men,
> so that you will not grow weary and lose heart.*
>
> Hebrews 12:1–3 (emphasis added)

Get it? "Let us fix our eyes on Jesus, the author and perfecter." Let us get our eyes off ourselves. Then we can walk
toward freedom. In this chapter and in chapters 8 and 9, I want
to give you a glimpse of the abundant life that is ours, through
Christ, because of who God is and who we are in Christ.

I AM FREE TO ACCEPT GOD'S LOVE

Our preoccupation with ourselves can convince us that
God doesn't love us. Traveling the country I hear the same
story over and over again: "I can't believe that God loves me.
If you really knew me, you'd understand why I feel this way."
"I feel so lost. I hate myself!" Wallowing in mud uses up so
much energy, sapping our joy.

That self-absorption makes some of us feel as if we have
nothing to offer to the Christian family, so we retreat to a spiritual bed-rest and do nothing. And sometimes it convinces us
that our service to God will impress him and make us worthy of
his love. It happened to me. I used to feel so valuable to God
because I had such a high-profile job as cohost of *The 700 Club*.
On some level I sensed that God would approve of my life if I
kept working harder and harder and producing more and more.
On the surface it looked good, but it's not a very steady platform. If God's love for us and acceptance of us has to do with
our lovability or usefulness, our boat is sinking fast. Actually,
my service for God was a barrier to my relationship with him.

I think our self-absorption—our self-hate—steals our joy also because it destroys our relationships with other people; it makes us incapable of loving others. It's impossible to love others and hate yourself. When you become caught in the net of self-loathing, you can appear sweet and helpful but underneath is a cauldron of resentment. You may see that point in this poem I wrote:

"Excuse me sweetly," she did say,
"I am stubble, thou art hay."
"Excuse me nicely, if thou wilt
I am cotton, thou art silk."
"Excuse me please," she carried on
"Thou art new and I am worn."
"Excuse me one more time," she bowed
And disappeared into the crowd.
'Twas plain for all the world to see;
She hated life, so hated me.

When you feel that everyone around you is more capable, more attractive, more lovable, you may think that you esteem them higher but in reality you despise them. It's only when we can receive the love of God for ourselves that we can rejoice at the beauty of God in others.

For me, one of the most important keys for unlocking the joy of the Lord was facing the truth about myself. I am a sinner desperately in need of God. My value, my worth, my strength is in him. One of my greatest weaknesses used to be that I thought I was strong.

But now one of my greatest strengths is that I know that I'm weak apart from Christ. I know that as surely as I know my own face in the mirror. And God knows that. When I gave up and gave myself to God, when I told him how helpless and hopeless I was, God didn't cover or excuse a thing. He didn't disagree with me on one point; in fact, I had a feeling that there would be more digging out—more self-surrender—to come at a later date, but in my surrender he assured me that he loved me. He loved me knowing that it was all true. In my surrender I was able to *receive* his love; I was emotionally able to appropriate his value as mine. It is one of the great eternal paradoxes that when you finally realize your worthlessness, Christ's love and grace declare you worthy—but it is in him that we find ourselves and in him is our worth.

Disillusionment and delight walked hand in hand for me. I experienced tremendous disappointment with myself as I faced the truth about who I really am, but not far behind that was the overwhelming embrace of the One who knew more than any other that I am not worthy and who loves me anyway. What a huge relief!

I propose that the less room we give to loving ourselves or despising ourselves, the more room there is to love God. And there's an upward cycle that sets in, because it's impossible to love God and hate yourself. When you love God you love the things God loves. God loves you. It's embarrassing and uncomfortable to be loved when we feel that we should be despised, but God is God. He looks at you with your list of the things that disqualify you, tears up your list, and places a kiss on both cheeks. Why argue with God till the end of time? What a waste of a life. Put down your old picture and take home the new one that he has painted of you in Christ.

Turn your eyes upon Jesus—that frees you to receive the love he freely offers. Turn your eyes upon Jesus—that frees you to get off center stage and see yourself as God's beloved. Saint Bernard of Clairvaux charts out four steps we take in the process of losing ourselves and finding ourselves in God. Can you identify where you are in your journey?

> Step 1. We love ourselves for our own sake.
> Step 2. We love God for our own sake.
> Step 3. We love God for his sake.
> Step 4. We love ourselves for God's sake.

The joy is in step 4—when we understand that we are robed in his righteousness.

How much human misery would be alleviated if we would sit for a while with this truth and let it sink into our souls. There is rest to be found in surrendering our quest for significance to God, accepting what is true about our lives that we have no worth apart from Christ. And in that surrender and clarity of vision comes the most awesome truth of all. The God of the universe, whose Word spoke life into being and whose Word will cause this world to come to an end, values your life so much that he gave his Son to die in your place. That should bring us to our knees and give dignity to our souls.

I AM ABLE TO REPENT OF MY SIN AND CONFESS GOD'S TRUTH

In her book *Repentance: The Joy-Filled Life*, Basilea Schlink says, "The first characteristic of the kingdom of heaven is the overflowing joy that comes from contrition and repentance.... Tears of contrition soften even the hardest hearts."

She's identified a truth as old as the psalms. Remember? David's plea for God to restore the joy of his salvation is in the middle of Psalm 51, a psalm of repentance, where he is laying his transgressions before God and asking for mercy. Where does the psalm start? With the truth about God's love. "Have mercy on me, O God, according to your unfailing love; according to your great compassion blot out my transgression."

David was a man who let his sin break his heart. Verse 17 says, "The sacrifices of God are a broken spirit; a broken and contrite heart, O God, you will not despise."

Even after our initial conversion, many of us—like me—need to come to a deeper realization of our sin and unworthiness before Christ. This is often a painful realization of brokenness. It is taking all the ways we have disappointed ourselves—the big sins, the little sins, the sins that have been dumped on us by others—and giving them to God. It means throwing ourselves at his mercy. As Joel 2:13 says, "Rend your heart and not your garments. Return to the LORD your God, for he is gracious and compassionate, slow to anger and abounding in love."

Believe me, "rending your heart" can feel like you're rending your garment. I think of the woman who said that she was like a sweater made of fear; fear so much defined her that without it she would unravel. There's no way for joy to knit itself through her life until she is ready to shed the sweater and stand naked before God without it. We too often skip over this part about being broken before God.

Oswald Chambers notes: "The bedrock of Christianity is repentance. Strictly speaking a man cannot repent when he chooses; repentance is a gift of God. The old Puritans used to pray for the 'gift of tears.' If ever you cease to know the virtue of repentance, you are in darkness. Examine yourself and see if you have forgotten how to be sorry."

What does repentance mean and who needs to do it? Is repentance only for the willful acts of disobedience to God's commands? Repentance surely is required for willful wrongdoing. And repentance by definition calls us to change direction. Make amends. Set things right. As Aldous Huxley says succinctly: "If you have behaved badly, repent, make what amends you can and address yourself to the task of behaving better next time. On no account brood over your wrongdoing. Rolling in the muck is not the best way of getting clean."

But many of us are burdened more with the awareness of our inability to carry out our best intentions of following Christ. We don't intentionally rebel. Despite our best intentions we "fall short of the glory of God." We know the truth named in James 3:2: "We all stumble in many ways." We echo the words of Paul in Romans 7. Paul knows he's wearing Christ's robes of righteousness, and yet he admits: "I have the desire to do what is good, but I cannot carry it out. For what I do is not the good I want to do." Paul goes on with various versions of this quandary for a long paragraph. Finally he throws up his hands: "What a wretched man I am!" And yet he doesn't utterly despair. He turns his gaze to Christ. He continues: "Who will rescue me from this body of death?" And then he answers his own question: "Thanks be to God—through Jesus Christ our Lord!" Christ is the victory—through grace.

This "thanks be to God" can be ours as we continually confess—affirm—our humanity, our weakness, and our utter dependence on him, calling on his strength. Try it: Give him your weakness and let him prove his strength. Paul tried it: He asked God to take away some unidentified "thorn" that tormented him. God responded, "My grace is sufficient for you, for my power is made perfect in weakness." Paul further reflects: "That is why, for Christ's sake, I delight in weaknesses, in insults, in hardships, in persecutions, in difficulties. For when I am weak, then I am strong" (2 Corinthians 12:9–10)—in Christ. Because of "Christ's power"—not his own.

Try it every morning. George MacDonald said, "With every morn my life afresh must break the crust of self, gathered about me fresh."

I admit I have a temper. I also know that it's hard for me to tell my husband off when I'm consciously saying—every morning—"God, this day, I acknowledge my dependence on you. This day I give my anger to you." I used to think, *I can't help it. This is just who I am.* I know now that is a lie from the enemy. I get to choose how to live. I am not a victim. I choose to live with intentionality, aware of my weakness apart from Christ but bringing it to him constantly.

God can use that daily—hourly—acknowledgment of our weakness to build a hedge around us—that guards us from stumbling into some huge pits. I say this because so many Christian women stumble into painful, harmful acts of sin because they are blinded by a self-righteous pride that makes them think they're "above" sin. I talked recently to a woman who had been respected in her church. She was responsible for the women's ministry and led the choir. "I've always been the 'good girl,'" she said. "When I would counsel women who had committed adultery, I would thank God that I was not like that.

And then it happened. I committed adultery. I was so blind to the possibility that I didn't even see it coming."

I thought about her words for a long time. I could relate so well to her sentiment that she was above certain sins. The truth is that none of us is above any sin. There is an arrogance in thinking that we are—an arrogance that comes because we do not continually remember our reliance on God and confess our weakness and faults before him.

Nothing alienates the secular world faster than Christian self-righteousness pseudo-holiness. We set ourselves up as being above the crowd and imagine that will make them flock to our doors. People can see through that thin veneer very quickly. The true message of the gospel is that there are no good people, only a good God who builds a bridge for sinners to cross.

Paul warns: "If you think you are standing firm, be careful that you don't fall!" He continues, "No temptation has seized you except what is common to man." (We're all in this together.) "And God is faithful; he will not let you be tempted beyond what you can bear" (1 Corinthians 10:12–13).

Take a deep breath and soak in the truth of these verses, written to Christians by the apostle John:

> *If we claim to be without sin, we deceive ourselves and the truth is not in us. If we confess [acknowledge the truth of] our sins, he is faithful and just and will forgive us our sins and purify us from all unrighteousness. If we claim we have not sinned, we make him out to be a liar and his word has no place in our lives. My dear children, I write this to you so that you will not sin. But if anybody does sin, we have one who speaks to the Father in our defense—Jesus Christ, the Righteous One. He is the atoning sacrifice for our sins, and not only for ours but also for the sins of the whole world. We know that we have come to know him if we obey his commands.*
>
> 1 John 1:8–2:3

Read it again. He is faithful to forgive.

Within the last year someone asked me if I'd seen a particular movie. I don't know why but I said, "Yes, I did. It was great." But I hadn't. I quickly changed the subject, struck by the horror of what I'd done. Why would I say something that wasn't true? I questioned myself for days about it. Perhaps I wanted to feel included or knowledgeable. I could have skipped over it or smiled at it as if it's just a little quirk of my humanity, but instead I found freedom and grace in confessing it as sin and receiving forgiveness.

In chapter 3 we discussed the difference between guilt and shame—guilt being caused by our awareness that we have *done* something wrong, shame convincing us that we *are* something wrong. How does this talk of repentance and confession help us break through the underlying distortions that tell us that we are loathsome creatures?

Remember Paul's telling exclamation: "wretched man that I am!" (Romans 7:24 RSV)? That's followed by his "thanks be to God" and then a one-verse acknowledgment of his good intent: "So then, I of myself serve the law of God with my mind, but with my flesh I serve the law of sin" (7:25 RSV).

Then Romans 8 starts with a wonderful line: "Therefore, there is now no condemnation for those who are in Christ Jesus." No condemnation.

Remember this: In Hebrew Satan means "accuser." And Revelation 12:10 names him as the accuser of those redeemed by Christ and living under his righteousness. The accuser is not out for our best interests. He rejoices in our defeats, in our discouragement, depression, and shame. He rejoices when he gets us to believe the lies. But he does not have the last word. Scripture addresses the lies that wrap us in shame: "This then is how we know that we belong to the truth, and how we set our hearts at rest in his presence whenever our hearts condemn us. For God is greater than our hearts, and he knows everything" (1 John 3:19–20). What is the "this then" referring to? It draws us back to love and to truth: "Dear children, let us not love with words or tongue but with actions and in truth" (v. 18).

John draws us out of the lies, asking us to live in love, to live in truth—as we rest in and live out the love God has given us. John calls us to love others in and with sincerity and truth that comes only as we appropriate God's love ourselves.

It's hard to spend more than ten minutes with Christ through his Word and not be impacted by the way his very life and presence banish shame. It's not that shame would be inappropriate for the human race; it's that Jesus took it all on himself for us. That's the key to Hebrews 12:2–3: "Let us fix our eyes on Jesus, the author and perfecter [finisher] of our faith, who for the joy set before him endured the cross, scorning its shame, and sat down at the right hand of the throne of God. Consider him who endured such opposition from sinful men, so that you will not grow weary and lose heart."

I HAVE PERMISSION TO GRIEVE

Grief—can it be a gateway to joy? Yes. A repentant heart allows us to grieve for our own sins; and a heart near to God can grieve for the havoc that sin has wreaked on humanity— even ourselves. Read the psalms of David. He's called a "man after God's heart" and, as Richard Foster says in his book *Prayer:* "Almost every page of the Psalter is wet with the tears of the singers."

I meet women all the time who say, "I'm afraid to cry.... I'm afraid that if I start, I'll never stop." There's so much pain dammed up that they're afraid of what will happen if they let a bit of water out. It's the pain of disappointment—maybe with themselves—but often with others. The pain of rejection. The pain of loss.

I shared a platform with a speaker who said something that was intended to be inspiring, but I couldn't clap with the crowd. She told us about a woman who had written her about the death of her child. The letter basically said, "I have your tapes and I've been able to move on without grieving because I have victory in Jesus." My heart grieved for this woman's lack of grief. Why did the audience clap? I think like Pavlov's dogs we are preconditioned in our Christian culture to respond to something that sounds inspiring and is delivered with emotion whether it's true or not.

It reminded me of a passage in *The Confessions of Saint Augustine*. Augustine and his mother, Monica, were very close. You might say she had prayed him into the kingdom, staying on her knees until her wayward son found his peace in Christ. And throughout his ministry she was there with him and for him. In writing about her death, he said, "But when she breathed her last, the boy Adoentus [Monica's grandson] burst into a loud lament; then checked by us all, held his peace." He continues, "And behold the corpse was carried to the burial; we went and returned without tears . . . yet was I the whole day in secret heavily sad." As you read on it's clear that Augustine felt it would be a poor witness to cry for his mother, for the loss of the physical presence of someone he loved dearly. God doesn't ask that of us.

God doesn't ask you or me to be the kind of woman who could bury a child or a parent with hardly a tear and then march off singing, "I'm in the Lord's army."

The Son of God was called "a man of sorrows," who was "familiar with suffering" (Isaiah 53:3). The King James Version uses the phrase "acquainted with grief." Christ wept when the occasion (the death of his friend Lazarus) called forth emotion. If the Son of God can let the overflow of his heart spill down his face, then so can we.

There may be appropriate and inappropriate times and places for allowing oneself to work through the grief of the losses of our lives, but holding the sorrow in for fear that "I'll never stop crying" is like a woman trying to hold a child in her womb when its time is come. It's pointless. It's harmful. It's preventing any hope of the joy that comes with the birth of a baby that is fruit of your womb. I remember when the first real pain of labor hit me with Christian. I had never faced anything like it, but without the pain and the breaking free there would have been no life for my son. I needed twenty-three stitches and I limped for a couple of months after his birth because a muscle had been nicked, but it was a pain that produced such joy. It seemed appropriate to me that there should be a fine scar left as a reminder of the process.

In his book *Prayer*, Richard Foster says all this sorrow and weeping—over our own sins or the sins of others—"sounds a bit depressing, at least to those of us who have been raised on a religion of good feelings and prosperity. The old writers, however, had a very different view.... For them the people most to be pitied are those who go through life with dry eyes and cold hearts."

I propose that joy is found only as you face and walk through your grief. For some, working through this emotion requires real courage. Søren Kierkegaard said, "It requires moral courage to grieve." But then he identified a second kind of courage, which I think comes along behind: "It requires religious courage to rejoice." I challenge you to "fix your eyes on Jesus," give him your pain, your disappointment, and trust it to him—in faith that he will take it on himself. In faith that "Those who sow in tears will reap with songs of joy" (Psalm 126:5). In faith that "weeping may remain for the night, but rejoicing comes in the morning" (Psalm 30:5).

Give your pain to God. Let go of it! We can become so defined by our trauma that we feel naked without it. God will give you a new suit of clothes to wear. Isaiah prophesied the coming of Christ who would "comfort all who mourn, and provide for those who grieve in Zion—to bestow on them a crown of beauty instead of ashes, the oil of gladness instead of mourning, and a garment of praise instead of a spirit of despair" (61:2–3). New clothes!

I like the line in one of Carly Simon's songs: "There's more room in a broken heart." It's amazing what God can do with the broken pieces of your life if you'll let him.

But thou wilt sin and grief destroy;
That so the broken bones may joy
And tuned together in a well set song

Full of his praises
Who dead men raises
Fractures well cured make us more strong.

George Herbert

I HAVE COURAGE TO GROW IN TRUTH

I started this chapter with a "lettuce" lineup found in Hebrews 12: "*Let us* throw off everything that hinders and the sin that so easily entangles, and *let us* run with perseverance the race marked out for us. *Let us* fix our eyes on Jesus. . . ."

First Peter 2:1–3 gives another twist to the theme, being specific about some of the hindrances that bog us down. "Rid yourselves of all malice and all deceit, hypocrisy, envy, and slander of every kind." Did you get that? We are to rid ourselves of deceit and hypocrisy. He continues: "Like newborn babies, crave pure spiritual milk, so that by it you may grow up in your salvation, now that you have tasted that the Lord is good." Peter assumes that we have tasted the goodness of the Lord, and on that foundation he says we can and should grow in our salvation.

It's such a joy to watch baby Christian learn new things. He's a quick study. I watched him studying his grandfather one night as he clapped during a televised ball game; then Christian joined in. We all laughed and clapped along. My mom taught him how to throw kisses, and he now throws kisses to all—from the pizza delivery guy to those behind us in line in the grocery store. We all get a huge kick out of it. I love to see him learn, and I get joy from seeing his joy when he makes a new discovery. This gives me a tiny living parable of the joy that must come to the heart of God when we learn and mature in our faith. It doesn't make him love us any more, but it brings him joy. What a wonderful thought that we can bring joy to the heart of God. "[The Lord] will take great delight in you, he will quiet you with his love, he will rejoice over you with singing" (Zephaniah 3:17).

Like Peter, Paul also uses the image of children growing to maturity. And both apostles write of maturity in terms
of living in the truth. Ephesians 4:14–16 says, "Then we will
no longer be infants, tossed back and forth by the waves, and
blown here and there by every wind of teaching and by the cun-
ning and craftiness of men in their deceitful scheming. Instead,
speaking the truth in love, we will in all things grow up into him
who is the Head, that is, Christ. From him the whole body,
joined and held together by every supporting ligament, grows
and builds itself up in love, as each part does its work."

We have this idea that being mature in Christ means we
do things for him. But I think growing in Christ has a lot to
do with living with increasingly less dissonance between what
we feel we are and who we tell the world we are. Living with
more truth and less hypocrisy.

On the one hand, we are growing more Christlike. The
epistles are full of exhortations of what we should lay aside—
and as we delight in the love and faithfulness of God, we find
there is joy in his precepts. (Check out Psalm 19:8: "The precepts of the LORD are right, giving joy to the heart. The commands of the LORD are radiant, giving light to the eyes.") We
find ourselves setting our hearts on doing right. As it says in
the 1 John 2, if we love him, we will obey him.

On the other hand, we are more transparent in our weakness. Our awareness of God's love for our humanity drives us
to trust him enough to quit hiding—as we look to Christ for
strength to walk in the truth, with confidence that we are covered with his righteousness, with his love, faithfulness, and hope.

I've already mentioned the powerful family drama played
out in the movie *Secrets and Lies*. At one point the main male
character, Maurice, breaks the silence and names one family
secret—not a gross sin, simply a human frailty and a cause of
great embarrassment and pain. He pauses. Then he says,
"There, I said it. So where's the bolt of lightning?" He pauses
again, and then he gives a little speech. "Secrets and lies. We're
all in pain. Why can't we share our pain?"

Getting the secrets out into the open was painful for everyone. But only then could conversation start and healing begin. Those secrets lost their power over a whole family.

Remember those fig leaves pitifully pinned on Adam and Eve? We're still hiding—behind secrets and sometimes lies. Sometimes because the truth is not dramatic enough and we thrive on chaos and the attention it brings. Sometimes we lie to hide our needs and vulnerability. We lie to avoid pain. Whatever the reason, it must be shown the door. "Do not lie to each other, since you have taken off your old self with its practices and have put on the new self, which is being renewed in knowledge in the image of its Creator" (Colossians 3:9–10). Pray daily that God would help you speak the truth—in love. If you fall, confess it and ask for forgiveness. You are a new creation in Christ. You don't have to be subject to behaviors from the past. You are not a victim; you are a child of the King, being renewed in knowledge in the image of your Creator.

In his book *The Art of Passingover*, Francis Dorff describes a process of spiritual maturity that progresses through three stages, which he calls "faces": "the face of nothing to prove," then we grow into "the face of nothing to hide," and finally we shine with "the face of nothing to fear." Let's look at what it means to have nothing to hide and nothing to fear.

Nothing to Hide

Growing into "the face of nothing to hide" from ourselves and our God, "we begin to experience an inalienable Freedom which changes our face from within. We begin singing, and living a completely new song," writes Dorff.

And this inner honesty allows us to be more honest with others. More often than not, the telling of your secret becomes a bridge over the gulf of your loneliness to someone else who feels just the same way and thought she was alone too. Dorff notes, "This does not mean that we are given to inappropriate self-disclosure. We know from experience that sort of psycho-spiritual 'show and tell' can do tremendous violence to the delicate inner reality of our own lives and the lives of others." I don't recommend standing on a street corner and proclaiming to Saturday morning shoppers that you have lustful thoughts; a little wisdom is called for! Find someone safe and as Scripture says in James 5:16: "Confess your sins to each other and pray for each other so that you may be healed."

In a Bible study recently we were asked to split into groups of three and confess to each other what we were struggling with most at that moment. Two other girls and I (yes, I know I'm forty-one) found a quiet corner and sat and looked at each other for a few moments.

I wonder what was happening in that period of silence. We'd been asked to search our hearts, but I expect the others—as well as I—had to have a minute to work through our fear of allowing ourselves to be vulnerable. You know the feeling? I return again to a favorite theme of mine, perfectly articulated by Miriam Adeney in *A Time for Risking:* "I am convinced that the great need of women today is to know the love of God and experience it deeply. *Only God's love is hot enough to melt our inhibitions*" (italics mine).

Finally I spoke up. "At the moment the thing I'm struggling with most is anger. I lose it so easily." Both girls began to cry and confessed that they too were struggling in this area. Honest confession liberates us from isolation and gives others permission to be real.

As we become more honest with ourselves, we become willing and able to share with others our hopes, dreams, regrets, struggles, and pain.

I think of a conversation I had with a friend when we were cooking in my kitchen. "That's why I hate Christmas!" she exclaimed—out of the clear blue.

I turned to look at her and said, "Sorry, I must have missed something there. Why do you hate Christmas?"

"Oh, it's just so commercial!"

"And?" I continued.

"What do you mean 'and'? Isn't that enough?" she said as she tossed chicken breasts in a marinade.

"Sure, it's enough," I replied. "But I don't believe that's the real reason you hate Christmas."

We washed our hands, picked up our coffee mugs, and sat down.

"Okay. The reason I hate it is that it's one more visible sign that my family doesn't really know me," she said, tears in her eyes.

"What do you mean?" I asked.

"Well, every gift I open says to me that those I grew up with, and spent the first third of my life with, don't even know what I like." She paused for a moment. "It's not that the gifts are dumb. It's that they are the wrong kind of dumb gifts. It hurts me to think they don't know me well enough to get me the right kind of dumb gifts."

All sorts of images floated through my mind. I thought of a family member of mine. In my early, contemporary Christian music days, I think she decided "she's different from me, so if I hate something, she will like it." What did this person think I liked? Green neon socks with flashing music staffs and purple earrings that dragged on the floor behind me as I walked!

"I know what you mean," I said, smiling. To me the memories were funny. I used to look forward to opening these gifts to see what else I could donate to the Elton John museum. But to my friend these memories had cut deeply into her heart. We talked for a long time about the risk of love, the risk of telling people who you really are. We talked about our desire for someone to see right into our souls and accept what is there.

"I feel lonely a lot of the time," she continued bravely. "But those 'special' times of the year seem to heighten the feeling for me."

"Have you ever said anything about how you feel?" I asked.

"No!" she replied as if I'd suggested shooting her grandmother.

"So you want them to know you better, but you won't let them into the building?"

"I guess I want them to know me without me having to tell them," she responded.

Being honest is especially difficult with our families, as they often have clear ideas of who they want us to be. Another friend of mine hasn't spoken to his mother in seventeen years. He's afraid of her. We've talked about the situation at length. "She's just too controlling," he says. "I can love her better from a distance." (I wonder if she feels better loved?)

We feel guilty if we have negative feelings toward our families, and so we stuff them and then wish we could stuff our families! True love demands a different approach. Honesty. I don't mean the "let's go on the Geraldo Rivera show so that I can tell you in front of a gawking nation that you ruined my life" approach. I mean loving, ongoing truth. I mean taking risks with one another and enduring some difficult moments because we want real relationship. Being honest *is* hard work and requires that we get a handle on the fears that keep us bound.

Nothing to Fear

Dorff's third stage, "the face of nothing to fear," is intricately connected to having nothing to hide. Dorff says the face of nothing to fear "radiates a youthful courage, joy and vitality. It is a face that knows what it means to live creatively through the experience of dying, again and again. It is a peaceful, benevolent face which carries a quiet smile, even in the most trying situations."

This fearless face, he says, "does not mean that we are never afraid again; it means that we have become accustomed to facing our fears, naming them, and being delivered from them."

Think about your fears. How many of the feared disasters never actually came to pass, or if they did, how many of them really were more than you could handle? Mark Twain said, "I am an old man and have known a great many troubles, but most of them never happened." We waste a great deal of energy dreading devastation that often never happens.

Sometimes our fears do come to pass. I lived for years flanked by fears like a flock of black vultures. "What if I fail?" "What if I let God and others down?" "What if I lose my ministry?" Yes, I lost it. When all my fears came to pass and performed their merry dance around me, I was blown all over the place, but when the wind was finally quiet I was still here and God still loved me.

One woman who lives with chronic depression recently identified an underlying fear that drained her energy and joy and made her hide from others. Tired of living with the nagging emotion, she asked herself a direct question, *What are you afraid of?* After much thought she named the monster. *I'm afraid someone will yell at me.* Well, so? Naming the fear helped her see that "someone might yell at me" is not exactly a reason to hide from the world.

I've already described a friend who was living under what he perceived to be the heavy burden of baldness. His self-loathing compounded by fear of what people would think of him if they "knew" he was bald made him a pitiable sight. (He wasn't fooling anybody.) I have to tell you the rest of the story—and what happened when both he and I were willing to take a risk for the sake of truth.

I could hardly bear to see this man living out his life with so little joy, trying so futilely to cover up his own humanity. I didn't know what to do. For a while I did nothing, not wanting to wound him. But eventually, when I heard others snickering behind his back, I took a risk of my own. I love this friend and hated the fact that what he was doing to "save face" was not working. I wanted him to be free and yet dreaded that I would make it worse for him. Finally I chose to speak out when I put myself in his position and knew that I would want him to speak the loving truth to me. We went for a walk on the beach and I said, "Tom, I don't think you have to do that with your hair. You have a great face, and I think you'd look cool without combing it over." We talked for a long time about how he dreaded admitting defeat and cutting his last long lock.

"What's the worst thing that could happen?" I asked him.

"I'd be bald!" he said.

"Okay. So what else?" I continued.

"What else do you need? That's bad enough. . . . I'd look like my dad!"

I laughed at that, grateful that Tom had made my point for me.

"I like your dad," I said. "One of the things I like most about him is that he's comfortable in his own shoes or with his own bald head!"

Tom smiled. "You're right. He is pretty cool." We hugged each other and went for pizza.

Next Sunday Tom showed up at church without his hair. He looked great! He also looked relieved, and that is the whole point.

"I feel a little naked," he confessed. "And my head's cold!" I laughed at his joke, knowing that one large hair does not a sweater make. "Most of all I feel free," he said.

This breakthrough called for courage for both of us. He faced what he was afraid of, embraced it, and was still standing at the end. Facing any fear—whether it's a fear of what others will say about us or a fear of hurting someone by telling the truth—is not a journey for the faint of heart. And sometimes, especially when the issues are complex or deep, counseling can be helpful. We sometimes need professionally trained help so that we can see the issues with clarity.

Courage doesn't come in a gift box from heaven. Courage is an on-the-road thing. Remember the Cowardly Lion in *The Wizard of Oz?* He was sure he had to get to the Emerald City to ask the Wizard for courage in a box. He was afraid of everyone and everything and he spoke really loudly to cover his cowardice. (A lot of people who yell and scream at others are scared stiff inside.) What the lion found was that *in the going was the becoming.* He was waiting around for courage, but it was inside him all the time. As he pushed on through the Forest of Fears toward the Emerald City, he found that courage had been his all along.

I think we misunderstand what courage is. It's not the absence of fear; it's the presence of God in the midst of fear.

If you are quaking in the presence of fear—of others, of vague insecurities of the future, of befalling disaster—I challenge you to turn to one of my favorite psalms—91.

> He who dwells in the shelter of the Most High will rest in the shadow of the Almighty. I will say of the LORD, "He is my refuge and my fortress, my God, in whom I trust." Surely he will save you from the fowler's snare and from the deadly pestilence. He will cover you with his feathers, and under his wings you will find refuge; his faithfulness will be your shield and rampart. You will not fear the terror of night, nor the arrow that flies by day, nor the pestilence that stalks in the darkness, nor the plague that destroys at midday. A thousand may fall at your side, ten thousand at your right hand, but it will not come near you. You will only observe with your eyes and see the punishment of the wicked. If you make the Most High your dwelling—even the LORD, who is my refuge— then no harm will befall you, no disaster will come near your tent. For he will command his angels concerning you to guard you in all your ways; they will lift you up in their hands, so that you will not strike your foot against a stone. You will tread upon the lion and the cobra; you will trample the great lion and the serpent. "Because he loves me," says the LORD, "I will rescue him; I will protect him, for he acknowledges my name. He will call upon me, and I will answer him; I will be with him in trouble, I will deliver him and honor him. With long life will I satisfy him and show him my salvation."

What a beautiful psalm! These promises are given to those who "rest in the shadow of the Almighty." This is the assurance of those who will bury their faces in God. On the next sunny day go out and take a look at how closely your shadow follows you; a shadow sticks right with the one it is reflecting. It doesn't have an opinion of its own. It doesn't have its own agenda. Wherever you go it follows you. This is a picture of the life secure in Christ. It's a life that has surrendered control and personal ambition and has nothing to prove, nothing to hide, and nothing to fear. The one who is at rest in God is not destroyed by the winds of this world, because that person has finally found what faith looks like and has taken her hands off the steering wheel.

Courage and fear are strange bedmates. It would seem to be impossible to have one and have the other too, and yet I believe that is the challenge of the Christian life. Courage and fear belong together. Fear tells us that life is unpredictable, anything can happen; courage replies quietly, "Yes, but God is in control." As Oswald Chambers said, "When you fear God you fear nothing else, whereas if you do not fear God, you fear everything else."

Note this wonderful exhortation by D. Martyn Lloyd-Jones:

> We must not think of ourselves as ordinary people. We are not natural men; we are born again. God has given His Holy Spirit, and He is the Spirit "of power and love and of a sound mind." Therefore to those who are particularly prone to spiritual depression through timorous fear of the future, I say in the Name of God and in the words of the Apostle: "Stir up the gift," talk to yourself, remind yourself of who you are, and of what spirit is within you; and having reminded yourself of the character of the Spirit, you will be able to go steadily forward, fearing nothing, living in the present, ready for the future, with one desire only, to glorify Him who gave His all for you.

Every time I feel fear rising inside me, I remember God. I memorize Scripture verses and tuck them in my soul. When I give into fear, I ask God to forgive me and to fill me with a fear of him alone.

GETTING TO JOY

1. Think of all the things that are true about your history that you think would disqualify you from God's love.

Write it all down. I find it helpful to see things in print and to be held accountable to what is before me. Remember that God knows every one of these things and loves you completely.

2. As you face some of the things that are true about your life, it might help you to have a phrase to repeat. I say, "I am a daughter of the King of kings! God is still on the throne and I am loved. There is nothing that will happen to me today that is a surprise to God."

3. Do you remember any of the "Disappointments with Myself" that you noted (and symbolically buried) after reading chapter 2? You might start there as you turn to God with a repentant heart. Acknowledge your sin and your failings and shortcomings—real and imagined—before God. Tell him of your desire to repent—turn from the past—with God's help.

4. Consciously, verbally confess the truth. Satan is not omniscient. He cannot read your thoughts, as God can, so say it out loud: "Satan, I refuse to accept the lies that you throw at my mind. I am a child of God and I live by the truth of Jesus Christ."

5. If you have lost a loved one, write a letter to that departed one. Pour out your heart, your grief and tears. When I was thirty seven I wrote a letter to my dad telling him how much I missed him, how often my thoughts turn to him. Even though I know he is home with the Lord, I found it healing to write the letter.

6. Here's what I do when I feel as if fear is getting a grip on me. Try it: I find a quiet, private spot, even if it's the bathroom. I close my eyes, take ten deep slow breaths, and say out loud: "The LORD is my light and my salvation—whom shall I fear? The LORD is the stronghold of my life—of whom shall I be afraid?" (Psalm 27:1). Sometimes at first I sound very unconvinced, so I say it again. I say it again and

again until I feel faith beginning to rise and occupy the space fear had held. You might also memorize these verses:

The LORD is with me; I will not be afraid. What can man do to me?
                                                            Psalm 118:6

God did not give us a spirit of timidity [fear], but a spirit of power, of love and of self-discipline.
                                                            2 Timothy 1:7

CHAPTER 8

THE JOY OF BEING FAITHFUL AND FREE

The truth will set you free.

John 8:32

Stone walls do not a prison make,
Nor iron bars a cage;
Minds innocent and quiet take
That for an hermitage;
If I have freedom in my love,
And in my soul am free,
Angels alone that soar above
Enjoy such liberty.

Richard Lovelace

J esus said the truth could—would—set us free. Free *from* fear, yes, and free to *be* all we were meant to be.

I HAVE A NEW CONVICTION TO BE AND TO BE ME

I used to struggle with Jesus' words to the Pharisees. He called them "snakes," "fools," "whitewashed tombs." As far as I could understand they were religious leaders who were doing their best to uphold God's law as they understood it. They lived their religious lives with greater intentionality than I have ever achieved. But if you take a second look, there are layers of great deception. They loved the place of honor at banquets and the best seats in the synagogue. They liked to be at the front of the parade. It is such an easy sin to fall into, it can even look godly.

But if you live on a pedestal, you spend half your time watching that you don't fall off. We can shore up our sad sense of self by building a "ministry" to support our sagging egos, or we can find ourselves by surrendering to God.

As you walk in the truth of who you are in Christ, you are empowered to "let go and let God." Sometimes we think that fifty-two things plus God matter, but the truth is that God matters and we matter to him, and that's about it. When your heart—not your head—grasps that truth, you can step out in the confidence of another biblical truth, found in Matthew 10:39: "Whoever finds his life will lose it, and whoever loses his life for my sake will find it." This sentence says "finding one's life" is possible—but only by finding it in him and only by throwing off our reliance on the extras. Let us keep our eyes on Jesus, not on what others will think of us.

A discussion of finding one's life, though grounded in Christ, must acknowledge that God has a unique place for *you*. Ephesians 2:10 says, "For we are God's workmanship, created in Christ Jesus to do good works, which God prepared in advance for us to do." Your works. Prepared for you.

In his book *Between the Dreaming and the Coming True*, Robert Benson relates the wisdom of a great Hebrew teacher. Rabbi Zusya once said, "In the world to come I shall not be asked: 'Why were you not Moses?' I shall be asked: 'Why were you not Zusya?'"

Benson continues, "The will of the One who sent us is that we be the one who was sent. What we do is meant to be lived out of the context of discovering and becoming the person we are."

As we progress through chapters 7, 8, and 9, we're shedding layers of "stuff." Layers of clothing that block the sun-rays of joy. We're getting closer to living as if Jesus' righteousness were all we need to walk faithfully and with faith. We're getting closer to being able to love that unique quality that is ours, like a child who could delight in the beauty of God and his creation.

I praise God that I no longer need to try to be Laura Bannerman. I can be Sheila Walsh and live out the truth of who I am.

I really like being me. I would much rather have ten people who really knew me and liked me than ten million who thought that they knew me but it wasn't the real me at all.

In her autobiography, Thérèse of Lisieux notes:

> The splendor of the rose and the whiteness of the lily do not rob the little violet of its scent nor the daisy of its simple charm. I realized that if every tiny flower wanted to be a rose, spring would lose its loveliness and there would be no wild flowers to make the meadows gay.

What are the things about you that are different from anyone else? The things you love about yourself—if you could just find them? Why did you "drop" them from your repertoire? Because they were different from everyone else? They're still there, you know, waiting to be drawn to the surface—showcased.

Maybe you need a little help drawing that hidden self into the reality of your daily routine. In her book *The Path*, Laurie Beth Jones suggests that we should all have a mission statement. A single sentence that clearly represents why we are on this earth. She says it should be simple enough for a child to understand but so burned into our souls that we could recite it by memory at gun point. Your mission statement says who you are, not just what you do.

I used to think that my mission was to be the cohost of *The 700 Club*. That was never my mission. That was my job. It gave room for me to fulfill my mission, but my mission went on after my job ended. As Eugene Peterson says in *Growing Up in Christ*, "A parent's main job is not to be a parent but to be a person." Our mission goes beyond our current role or task.

I have written a personal mission statement: *To learn to love God more and communicate his love to others.* Obviously the implications of that are vast, but in reality it says it all.

A mission statement is a faithful friend in many ways. It serves as a plumb line in a busy world. It gives us focus and clarity when we are pulled in different directions. What fits with our mission statement, we say "yes" to, and what does not, we leave for someone else.

Consider this reflection by Henri Nouwen, from his book *Can You Drink the Cup?*

> When we are committed to do God's will and not our own we soon discover that much of what we do doesn't need to be done by us. What we are called to do are actions that bring us true joy and peace. . . .
>
> Actions that lead to overwork, exhaustion, and burnout can't praise and glorify God. What God calls us to do we *can* do and do *well.* When we listen in silence to God's voice and speak with our friends in trust we will know what we are called to do and we will do it with a grateful heart.

One particular verse on prayer has become very important to me: "If any of you lacks wisdom, he should ask God, who gives generously to all without finding fault, and it will be given to him" (James 1:5). I'm sure that I must have read this verse over and over through the years, but I never took it seriously until about a year ago.

My life had been quiet for a while. I had taken time off from television and traveling to go back to school and deepen my roots. The slow and steady pace of my days was a welcome change from the frantic life I used to lead. But then things began to move again after the publication of my book *Honestly.* I was committed to traveling two weekends a month with the Women of Faith team. Soon other invitations started coming in like cats and dogs on a rainy day. I knew it would be foolish to return to the madness of former days, but how was I to discern which to accept? Yes, sometimes people giving invitations suggested I "pray about it," but in the past I had never taken that very seriously. As far as I was concerned any chance to sing or speak was a God-given opportunity, and I said yes. I said yes until it almost killed me.

One morning as I was sitting with a cup of tea, I asked God to help me. "Lord, I don't have a clue what to do here. I know that you don't want me to run around like a headless chicken, but how do I know what you want me to be involved with? I'd be grateful if when you answer this prayer you could make it really clear, because I am so full of my own ideas that a quiet whisper from you wouldn't stand a chance."

Later that week I was reading James, and I stopped at verse 5: "If any of you lacks wisdom, he should ask God, who gives generously to all without finding fault, and it will be given to him." It was one of those rare moments when I felt as if God had turned the sun onto the page. I got it so clearly that I cried out, "Of course! Thanks!"

Every day from then till now before every important telephone conversation or meeting or just at the beginning of a new day, I pray with total conviction, "Lord, you have said that if we lack wisdom, we should turn to you and ask for it. So here I am. You know me so well. I have no wisdom of my own. All I want to do are the things that make you happy, so, please, show me and I will do them with all my heart. Speak to me in the quiet of my heart. Let your *yes* be clear to me and give me ears to hear your *no*. When you say *no*, I will let it go and thank you for closing the door, and when you say *yes*, I will run to it with all my heart."

It would be easy to pray this prayer—the part about being thankful for closed doors—with the whine of a pseudo-martyr. (The old Sheila would have.) But now I understand! God knows what he is doing, and if he closes a door I should get down on my knees and worship, because to have walked through blindly would have resulted in pain to others or myself.

I AM READY TO DREAM, READY TO STAND, READY TO RUN

A young man stood limply in the doorway, a small case at his feet.

"Yes?" I asked, "can I help you?"

"I'm selling brushes," he said apologetically.

"Oh," I said, "what kind of brushes?"

"They're called Betterwear," he replied.

"And are they?" I asked.

"Are they what?"

"Better wearing," I said.

"I don't really know. That's just the name of the company."

Everything about him, from his posture to the look on his face, announced loudly, "Get your brushes somewhere else!"

I wanted to say to this guy, "Go back and read your company's manual. Perhaps you were home sick the day when they told the sales team how good these brushes are. I think you've missed the vision here."

Many of us miss the vision of who we can be, because we don't step out and dare to dream of a future that is founded on the love, faithfulness, and hope inherent in our God. "'I know the plans I have for you,' declares the LORD, 'plans to prosper you and not to harm you, plans to give you hope and a future'" (Jeremiah 29:11).

I expect that many of my readers are in the midst of "the middle years" of life, facing what might be called a "second call." After the nest is empty, then what? Or death may have caused a major transition, or sometimes a painful divorce. Brennan Manning says that there are three things that stand in the way of our embracing God's "second call" on our lives: a crisis of faith, a crisis of hope, a crisis of love.

Those who are able to catch a fresh vision for the future are those who are able to abide in and be empowered by the faithful God of love and hope. Are you ready to reach for the dream that will take you beyond your disappointments?

Ready to Dream

Whose dream are you living? Are you living *your* dream, or the one that someone else had for you? Our time on earth is limited, so why spend it living what someone else—a parent, a friend, a spouse—imagined for us? Why not get down to the dream God implanted in you and wants you to live out? Catch the vision!

There's a story told about Michelangelo walking down the street, pushing a very large rock. Some passerby asked him why he was taking such pains with just an old rock. The artist's answer? "There's an angel in this rock that wants to come out." What does the angel in your rock look like? What dream has God buried in you—ready for sculpting?

Step back in time for a moment. Whether you're seventy-five years old or twenty-five years old, for a moment see yourself at age eighteen, sitting in a graduation gown. Thousands of others are there with you, and no one knows who will be asked to make the student speech. Then someone walks up to you and says you've got ten minutes to prepare your speech on "My Life's Dream." You cry, "I can't write a speech in ten minutes! I can't speak in public. I don't do that sort of stuff." But you have no choice. You're up in ten minutes. You have to. So, here and now, lay aside all you think you can do and all you're convinced you can't and dream for a moment. If you could do anything in the world, what would it be? If you got to start all over again, what would you do? Do you remember the dreams you carried as a young girl, a young woman? What were the things that made you, you? What kind of mark did you want to leave on the world? Perhaps as an eighteen-year-old you didn't know Christ and now you do. How has he changed your vision for your life? What dream does God's Spirit spark in your spirit? Remember George Eliot's words: "It's never too late to be what you might have been."

To reclaim your dreams, start with your natural talents and gifts. In her book *The Eighth Day of Creation*, Elizabeth O'Connor proposes that "we cannot be ourselves unless we are true to our gifts. . . . Our obedience and surrender to God are in large part our obedience and surrender to our gifts." What are you good at? What do you feel passionately about? What do you love to do?

If someone gave you five million dollars and said, "This is a gift, do with it what you will," how would it change your life? If that happened to me, I would obviously have to ask God what to do with the money. (I expect I would pay off the mortgage, for starters.) But after that it wouldn't change my day-to-day life at all. I am doing what I love to do. I spend my days with my husband and baby. We all travel together. I get to speak to women about what I believe really matters in life. I read old and new books that I adore, and I write, which I would do whether anyone ever published a word of it or not. That's why I think of myself as a writer rather than an author, because writing is my passion.

What's yours? Have you always wanted to go back to school? Perhaps now is the time to do it. One of my girlfriends went through a very painful, unwanted divorce recently, but God met her in the midst of her despair, and she has taken a step out into the unknown and signed up for graduate school. She is scared stiff but more alive than I've seen her in some time.

Walt Kallestad, author of *Wake Up Your Dreams*, advises having a dream mate, "someone who believes in and respects you and helps you sort *the good* from the *better* or *best*." But he knows the importance of establishing your own dreams with and before God—not living out someone else's dream for you.

> We need to elicit credible feedback from others. At the same time, I caution you never to permit one person's disappointment to cancel your appointment with pursuing your dreams. Just as surely as the slightest bit of egg yolk, slipped in with the egg whites, spells death for a meringue, one simple comment that plants doubts in your mind can impair the entire dreaming process. If a teacher, parent, friend, or work associate tells you that you don't have what it takes, don't automatically accept that opinion as fact. . . .

If you feel God's call, keep going. God can—and does—speak as we move out and take the next step.

Start where you are and just do it! I'm often asked "How did you get started in the music world?" Or "How did you get published?" I took every opportunity made available to me no matter how small, and I did it because I loved it. Don't sit around waiting for a big break. Make little waves of your own, and God will put the wind into your sails.

Picture a small house surrounded with a white picket fence. There is a rose garden and a bird feeder. On the porch two rocking chairs are occupied by two white-haired ladies. Sally is visiting Mary.

Sally is full of stories. She talks of the adventures she has had and continues to have in God. Not everything was successful. There were failures and bruises and dark moments, but there was life every step of the way.

Mary listens quietly, smiles a little, and pours more tea. "You always were the one for adventures, Sally!" she says with a slight shake of her head.

"Yes," Sally replies, the creases around her eyes deepening as she smiles. "Life is good. God is good! Well, I must be off. I have some visitation to do. Take good care of yourself, Mary." She reaches over to hug her friend good-bye.

"I will," Mary says wistfully as Sally heads off down the path. "I always have."

When you face your own later years, which woman do you want to be like? The one who played it safe and has no runs in her hose, or the one who threw herself in, who threw open the windows to God and to the world and was covered in sunshine in the process? Sign me up, Sally!

In 1994 Nelson Mandela delivered his inaugural speech as president of South Africa. He obviously took more than ten minutes to write his speech, and he made some very good points. One thing he said was that our "playing small" doesn't serve the world at all. Many of us—especially women I think—

don't want to stand out or be different, so we play small. As you ask God to wake up your dream, I challenge you not to be afraid of being the only one in a room whistling "your song." If it's the right tune, keep whistling until someone else catches the melody.

Ready to Step and Stand

Sometimes our God-implanted dreams require real courage, the strength described by Isaiah: "Awake, awake, O Zion, clothe yourself with strength. Put on your garments of splendor, O Jerusalem. . . . Shake off your dust; rise up, sit enthroned, O Jerusalem. Free yourself from the chains on your neck, O captive Daughter of Zion" (52:1–2).

Let me give you a glimpse into the dream—and the courage—of a young Siberian woman whom I know through my friend Marlene.

In her late teens Lida Vashchenko longed for freedom to be able to worship Christ freely. To make that freedom a reality, she walked through her fear, got on a train to Moscow, and pushed her way through the gates of the American embassy, seeking asylum. When no one knew what to do with her, she began a hunger strike. After thirty days, at eighty pounds, she was taken from the embassy to a hospital. Weak and hardly able to stand, she was forced to stand in front of sixteen men in her underwear as they questioned her.

"Do you think at eighty pounds you can fight the entire Soviet nation?" a KGB officer asked her.

"No," she replied, "but I serve a God who can."

After seven years living as a virtual prisoner, Lida came to the United States. When Marlene asked her what it was like to live under that kind of intimidation, Lida replied, "It is better to die doing something for God than to live doing nothing at all."

Perhaps you think that those words are more credible on a movie screen than from the lips of a young Siberian woman, but it really all depends on where you are standing in life. When you become alive inside, really alive to the edges of heaven that invade our world all the time, what is there to be afraid of? When you know deep in the marrow of your bones that this life that we cling to is a mere shadow of our real lives that are hid, safe with God in heaven, there is a limit to what anyone can do to us. Hebrews 13:5–6 quotes two books of the Old Testament, adding a "confident" transition: "'Never will I leave you; never will I forsake you.' So we say with confidence, 'The Lord is my helper; I will not be afraid. What can man do to me?'" Exactly!

It's not too late. I think of a gospel story of Jesus healing a possessed boy. The desperate father says to Jesus, "If you can do anything, take pity on us and help us."

Jesus seems taken aback with the request. He answers with a question: "If you can?" (as if he couldn't believe what he'd heard). And then Jesus comes in with the clincher: "Everything is possible for him who believes."

"Immediately the boy's father exclaimed, 'I do believe; help me overcome my unbelief!'" (Mark 9:21–24). I like this man. I identify with him. I respect his honesty. He loved his boy and would try anything to help him. Everything is possible for him who believes in the God of hope.

Rekindle the dream God has implanted in your heart.

Ready to Run

God sometimes calls us to be fully our unique selves as we trust him to carry us down *new* roads—journeys that require so much faith that we are utterly dependent on him for any success.

I was very shy as a young girl and also suffered from motion sickness. I couldn't go for more than a few miles in a car without throwing up. Now I have traveled all over the world. It's not because I can, because I can't! It's because God can through me.

And as for public speaking—I was chosen once by our church to make a presentation speech to a favorite youth leader who was getting married. I practiced and practiced, but when I stood up in front of that small crowd in the hall of Ayr Baptist Church, I froze. I stood there in absolute silence before I blurted out, "We're all surprised you're getting married." I practically threw poor Elizabeth Burley's gift at her and then sat down. But now I have the privilege to stand before thousands of women and share my faith-story with them. Did I swallow Dale Carnegie's book *How to Win Friends and Influence People?* Did I take a speech course? No! I stepped out scared stiff, and there was God.

Did Moses feel competent to lead God's people to the Promised Land? No. He said, "O Lord, I have never been eloquent, neither in the past nor since you have spoken to your servant. I am slow of speech and tongue.... O Lord, please send someone else to do it" (Exodus 4:10, 13).

Did Jeremiah feel able to speak God's word to his generation? No. God said, "Before I formed you in the womb I knew you, before you were born I set you apart; I appointed you as a prophet to the nations." And Jeremiah answered, "Ah, Sovereign LORD, I do not know how to speak; I am only a child." And God's response? "Do not say, 'I am only a child.' You must go to everyone I send you to and say whatever I command you. Do not be afraid of them, for I am with you and will rescue you" (Jeremiah 1:5–8).

There's David facing Goliath, Peter walking on water, Deborah leading an army. Do you think they felt competent? Hardly. Perhaps you think you don't look like the one God would choose. "I am only a woman." Or you can think of several other women in your church who are obviously gifted. They're good at it, they love it, so sit back and let them do it. Is that what God wants?

Here's the scenario of Samuel discerning which son of Jesse was "fit" to be king of Israel. Seeing Jesse's oldest son, Eliab, Samuel thought, "Surely the LORD's anointed stands here before the LORD." But God said to Samuel, "Do not consider his appearance or his height, for I have rejected him. The LORD does not look at the things man looks at. Man looks at the outward appearance, but the LORD looks at the heart" (1 Samuel 16:6–7).

Samuel subsequently looked at a whole line of brothers and finally asked Jesse, "Are these all the sons you have?"

"There is still the youngest," Jesse answered, "but he is tending the sheep."

Samuel said, "Send for him."

When David came, God told Samuel, "Rise and anoint him; he is the one" (1 Samuel 16:11–12). Even Samuel the prophet would have picked the oldest brother. But God said no. God knows our hearts. God knows that we can't—but he can. All things are possible—if God is in them.

I encourage you to stop and pray this beautiful prayer by Ken Gire from his book *Windows of the Soul*. The prayer is aptly titled "A Prayer for Joy."

> *Help me, O God,*
> *To listen to what it is that makes my heart glad*
> *and to follow where it leads.*
> *May joy, not guilt,*
> *Your voice, not the voice of others,*
> *Your will, not my willfulness,*
> *be the guides that lead me to my vocation.*
> *Help me to unearth the passions of my heart*
> *that lay buried in my youth.*
> *And help me to go over that ground again and again*
> *until I can hold in my hands,*
> *hold and treasure,*
> *Your calling on my life . . .*

Amen!!!

GETTING TO JOY

1. Choose three words that you would like to describe you, such as courageous, outgoing, compassionate. Pray and dream toward these characteristics.

2. Write out a mission statement for your life. (The three words chosen for exercise 1 might be helpful in thinking about your personal statement.)

3. Imagine that you went to your mail box today and there was a check for five million dollars. It was bequeathed to you by an elderly woman with the only proviso being, "Go for your dream." What would you do? This can help you identify the passions of your heart.

4. Talk to family members or friends who knew you when you were younger. What do they remember about you that was special? Take the best of their insights and mull them over as you hone the dreams you set out to fulfill.

5. Find a dream mate who will help you see your strengths and sort out the *good* from *the better* and *the best*. Ask three good friends what they see as your strongest gifts.

CHAPTER 9

THE JOY OF
LOVING OTHERS

*As God's chosen people, holy and dearly loved, clothe yourselves
with compassion, kindness, humility, gentleness and patience.
Bear with each other and forgive whatever grievances you may
have against one another. Forgive as the Lord forgave you. And
over all these virtues put on love.*

Colossians 3:12–14

Remember the acronym J-O-Y? It whispers that Jesus-
Others-You is the secret to joy. Often, however, our self-
absorption or self-hate makes us incapable of loving others. It's
impossible to love others and hate yourself. If our eyes aren't
first on God and his abiding love, we can rush out and "serve"
for reasons that may have some merit, but they short-circuit
the joy of the Lord.

The Galatians 5 list of the fruit of the Spirit—love, joy,
peace—is preceded by a summary of the commandments. The
summary itself is found in the Old Testament; Leviticus 19:18
says, "Do not seek revenge or bear a grudge against one of your
people, but love your neighbor as yourself. I am the LORD." It's
as if we are being told not to bear a grudge against ourselves.
The "love your neighbor as yourself" summary is repeated several times by Jesus and also in the epistles of Romans, James,
and Galatians, where it leads into a discussion of the "acts of

the sinful nature" as contrasted to the fruit of the Spirit. "You, my brothers, were called to be free. But do not use your freedom to indulge the sinful nature; rather, serve one another in love. The entire law is summed up in a single command: 'Love your neighbor as yourself'" (Galatians 5:13–14).

Who is my neighbor? The gospel of Luke tells the story of a man who asked that very question of Jesus. In response Jesus told one of his best-known parables—the Good Samaritan. The ostracized foreigner reached out to help a robbed and wounded stranger. The neighbor was another person—another sinner—in need of God's love and grace.

In his book *With Open Hands*, Henri Nouwen says, "At the moment when you grant that God is God who wants to be your God, and when you give him access to yourself, you realize that a new way has been opened for the person who is beside you. He too has no reason to fear, he too does not have to hide behind a hedge. . . . The garden which has been unattended for so long is also meant for him." There is nothing exclusive about the grace granted you; God wants to share the blessing—and through you.

One day a college professor gave a difficult exam, which hardly anyone finished before the bell rang at the end of the hour. The professor gave an A to the star student who had finished, and at the next class he handed the papers back to the other students and told them they had a second chance— more time to finish the unanswered questions.

The professor was amazed at the reaction of the student who'd already received an A. The student got angry—it wasn't fair that the others should be given a second chance. "Wait a minute," the teacher said. "You got your A. It's on the record. So what's the problem with someone else getting more time— to finish answering the questions?"

Do you ever feel like that student? Afraid God might want to give everyone a blessing?

And are you ever afraid he might want to use you to be a part of the blessing?

I wonder if Judy ever asked that question. In *My Neighbor, My Self*, Elise Chase tells the story of her friend Judy, whose life reads like a whirlwind of activity: raising four children alone, taking in a Cambodian family, a destitute teenager, and others in transition. Where does she get her strength? Judy says,

> Whenever I get to thinking that maybe I'm at the center of this ... everything comes crashing down. It's God working through me, that's all. When you love Him totally—then everything just starts to change. It's really a love affair, you know. Once a month I go for the weekend to a retreat house by the ocean. Just veg out, there by the sea, and spend time with Jesus doing absolutely nothing. We go running down the beach together, He and I. And we laugh a lot, too. But you know, one thing I've got to say. You better not start saying *yes* unless you really want your life to be turned upside down. Because it's a very demanding love affair! You better know that right from the start. Once you get into that business of really beginning to love Jesus, you're not going to be the one in control.

Her comment reminds me of the story of Peter, encountering Jesus after the resurrection. If you remember, Peter has denied Christ. (I imagine that Peter's denial was itself part of the "shame" that Jesus endured at his crucifixion.) Peter has repented, and here Jesus asks Peter, "Do you love me?" Yes, Lord. Then "feed my lambs." "Do you love me?" Yes, Lord. Then "take care of my sheep." "Do you love me?" Yes, Lord. Then "feed my sheep." Jesus continues, cryptically saying that life for Peter is not going to be easy. "When you were younger you dressed yourself and went where you wanted; but when you are old you will stretch out your hands, and someone else will dress you and lead you where you do not want to go.... Follow me!" (John 21:18–19).

I think Peter doesn't quite get it, because he points to a fellow disciple and says, "What about him?"

Jesus replied, "What is that to you? You must follow me" (John 21:21–22).

Jesus says the same to us—if you love me, feed my sheep. And this assumes that God will give us something to feed them with—not that we will have to "create the food" ourselves.

This brings me right back to the J of J-O-Y. The fruit is ours to share as we abide in the true vine. And the true vine is also the Bread of Life—and there's enough to go around. "I am the living bread that came down from heaven," Jesus said. "This bread is my flesh, which I will give for the life of the world" (John 6:51).

Remember the account of the feeding of the five thousand? When one child opens his hand and gives God his small lunch—just look at what God does with it. Five thousand men (dare I call them "sheep"?) are fed when a boy "lets go" and lets God love through him.

Still afraid there might not be enough love to go around? In *My Neighbor, My Self*, Elise Chase quotes a friend who took in a neighbor's two children for a week—tending them along with her own five. By the end of the week, she was exhausted and frazzled. "The thing was, I *knew* God had called me to help out in this way, so I also knew he would give me the resources I needed. That allowed me really just to ask Jesus to love everyone *through* me. And as soon as I asked, I could feel Him giving me new strength."

I AM ABLE AND WILLING TO FORGIVE

Jesus gives us a clear command that our relationships are to be grounded in an attitude of forgiveness. He sets a high standard for his disciples: "For if you forgive men when they sin against you, your heavenly Father will also forgive you. But if you do not forgive men their sins, your Father will not forgive your sins" (Matthew 6:14–15). But sometimes we convince ourselves that we can't forgive. Charles Spurgeon said, "Let us go to Calvary to learn how we may be forgiven. And then let us linger there to learn how to forgive."

As I learn to rest in God's love for me and his faithfulness to me, I am able to let go of resentments and past hurts—

the pain of wounds that others have caused me. Some disappointments and resentments slough away as I become able to receive—internalize—the gift of God's love and as I fix my eyes on Christ, not on myself. Why? Because I'm learning the truth expressed so well by writer Marie Stendhal: "Almost all our misfortunes in life come from the wrong notions we have about the things that happen to us." In our self-absorbed world, we can quickly convince ourselves that everyone else is out to get us. And viewing ourselves as the center of attention can cause us to take offense when no offense was intended.

As I mentioned earlier, Marcus Aurelius said, "The most important thing that a man can choose is what he thinks." As I see it, we become the incarnation of our thoughts. That is a very strong statement, but I believe it more strongly than I can adequately express. Understanding this and breaking through this barrier can transform our lives. What do I mean by *incarnation?* I mean that so much of life is a self-fulfilling prophecy. It is true in many areas, but I'll focus on one. Too often we get in the habit of thinking, "Someone always does me wrong." We hear offense even when it's not intended—because of our negative thought patterns habits we've collected, lies we've believed, over a lifetime.

How do you change the habits of a lifetime? I love the line of Mark Twain: "You can't break a bad habit by throwing it out the window. You've got to walk it slowly down the stairs." Slowly and deliberately. Throwing something out of a window is easy. It's a one-time thing and it's done. Walking takes commitment. It takes the first step and the next and the next until you get to the door.

I highly recommend the book *The Lies We Believe* by Dr. Chris Thurman. He suggests a very practical way developed by psychologist Albert Ellis to defeat the lies we believe about ourselves and others.

Imagine a typical scenario. I'll pick what happened to me yesterday, when I had a haircut scheduled. The last time I had an appointment, they had overbooked my stylist; he wasn't able to take me. So this time I had been very careful to make sure I was written in properly. Or so I had thought! Actually, the receptionist called me at home and said, "I'm sorry, but Mark won't be able to take you. He's going out to style hair for a video."

So let's call my receiving that piece of news A—the event. That's quickly followed by B—what plays in my head. Which was, *I can't believe he's done this again! These people are idiots! This will ruin my whole week! Why does this always happen to me?* My "head trip" is followed by C—my emotional reaction—anger, frustration, disappointment.

How do we break this unhelpful cycle? We live in a world of human beings and these things are going to happen, but we don't have to be tossed around by every unintentional (or even intentional) "slight" against us. We can choose D and E. D says, *Let's try some truthful self-talk.* As for my hair stylist, I can tell myself, *That's inconvenient, but it's not the end of the world. I don't have to have my hair cut this week. I can be happy with my hair the way it is! Or perhaps I need to find a new salon as Mark seems too busy.* I don't have to take personal affront. In this scenario my emotional response (E) would be disappointment but not anger and self-pity.

Try writing down a few scenarios that would be typical for you. Perhaps it might be a conflict with your husband or a coworker. Sometime when you respond to a situation with anger or rage, wait until the dust has settled and write down what happened. Write down what went through your head and how you felt. Then write down what might have been more appropriate or accurate.

We get to choose whether we'll go through life with negative tapes playing over and over or whether we will replace them with the truth. It won't happen overnight. You can't throw such an established habit out of the window, you have to walk it down the stairs! We're called to a renewing of our minds. "Do not conform any longer to the pattern of this world, but be transformed by the renewing of your mind. Then you will be able to test and approve what God's will is—his good, pleasing and perfect will" (Romans 12:2).

This practice of walking a negative thought pattern down the stairs can short-circuit a lot of anger that causes guilt and then calls for forgiveness. Ultimately, getting our eyes off our sorry selves, we naturally give more grace to others and have less "offense" to forgive.

But sometimes we are more convinced that the problem isn't ours. Someone does us wrong, and we feel let down, disappointed, betrayed. How do we get to forgiveness when someone has cut us to the heart?

First, forgiveness does not happen overnight. If wounds are deep, we must allow ourselves time to grieve. Someone's sin against you is breaking God's heart, and God knows that it's breaking yours. Let God's grief cover your first shock of betrayal.

In a *Today's Christian Woman* article titled "When Forgiveness Seems Impossible" (November/December 1984) Patricia Gundry walks through "the beginning stages of forgiveness," when

> we tend to blame people—ourselves, the offending party, and even God. There is no need for guilty feelings about this blame laying, as it is only an outworking of our beliefs that good people who do the right things at the right time don't get hurt; that only bad people go around causing others pain; and, over and above all, that God shouldn't have allowed this to happen to us, because we did not deserve it at all.
>
> But we do not understand that it may have happened to us precisely because we didn't deserve it. If we had, we might have seen it coming and ducked. Part of reconciling belief systems with reality may involve understanding that those who victimize often seek those of us who don't suspect we will be hurt. And we don't suspect wrongdoing because we are trusting, honorable, loving, and naïve people.

We do not want to believe that those whom we had trusted have been capable of digging a knife into us all along. Were we a poor judge of character? Or we may be angry or disappointed with ourselves because we did have suspicions which we foolishly discounted. But if we can allow ourselves to process this new information without hurry or guilt, new insights will enrich us as well as help heal our wounds.

If we can understand that the evil, cruelty, carelessness, or dishonesty in these people are only *parts* of their own value systems and not wholly *them*, we can come to another step in our progress toward healthy and genuine forgiveness.

In his book *The Art of Forgiving*, Lewis Smedes lays out three stages of forgiving. He starts with this last point of Gundry's: *We forgive as we rediscover the humanity of the offending party*. When we have been deeply wounded by someone, we tend to see that person as if she *were* the offense; she becomes defined for us in terms of the act committed against us. Blinded by our pain, we don't see the person.

When I am hurt by someone, I try to think of other aspects of that person's life. Who is she aside from her offense to me—her lie or brutish selfishness? I see this person as a son or as someone's mother. Maybe as a wounded person not knowing how to ask for help.

In the middle of the night I once answered the phone and listened as a friend asked for help, because she had taken an overdose of pills. I rose to the occasion, drove her to the emergency room, and sat there for three hours, praying, sipping a cup of vending machine coffee—until a doctor came out and asked to talk with me. "Why did you bring your friend in tonight?" he asked.

Thinking it a very strange question I replied, "Because she took an overdose of pills. She was staggering when I got to her door."

"She didn't take anything," he told me. "You can take her home."

I couldn't believe it. I was angry and felt betrayed. Driving home in the rain at 5 A.M., we sat in silence. Then I asked, "Why? Why did you pretend to have taken pills? Why would you lie about something like that? I was worried sick about you."

"I don't feel important to you anymore," she said.

It took me some time to work through the anger I felt. I thought, *Why wouldn't you just say to me that you don't feel important to me anymore?* But when I took a step back, I saw more. My friend finds it hard to express herself. That's who she is. Looking at her through the window of her humanity helped me to forgive her. We all respond differently and need space and grace to grow. When I want to harbor resentment against someone, I try to enlarge my picture and be prepared for God to soften my heart.

Forgiveness has been a hard lesson for me to learn, and I continue to be challenged to go deeper and give God permission to work in me.

Smedes says a second stage of forgiveness is *surrendering our right to get even*. There is something buried into the makeup of our souls that makes us cry for justice. Letting go of our right to get even is hard, difficult work. It comes as we relinquish ourselves to God, as we take responsibility for how we responsibly *react* to someone's offense—not "getting back." To forgive we have to surrender the desire to play God.

A coworker once hurt me very badly. I felt betrayed and lied about and astonished by this person's commitment to wound me. I struggled daily between two poles: feeling God's call to forgive him and wanting him to suffer. I wanted him to suffer, and I wanted him to know it was because of what he had done to me. I knew that I had to let go of my right to get even—but I fought it. "It's so unfair!" I cried over and over like a petulant child, even as God patiently reminded me of his grace to me.

Smedes says the third stage of forgiveness is *revising our feelings*. By God's grace, I could eventually begin to pray God's blessing on my coworker. I remember the day when I heard that something bad had happened to him. I felt such an ache for him. By that point I saw him as someone just like me, desperately in need of the mercy of God. My childish desire for him to fail had been replaced by a fresh understanding of God's grace to me. We don't know what's going on behind the scenes with one another, and we judge so quickly on the little information we have. Thank God that he who knows all also loves.

Are this former coworker and I good friends now? No. But I can say that I hold no animosity toward him. Old resentments that drained me of energy and joy are gone.

Forgiving someone does not necessarily mean you trust that person. I think of one woman who recently left her husband who had been beating her for more than five years. Twice he had broken her nose. She had to have her jaw wired after one right hook. Finally she ran. But her pastor told her that if she had really forgiven her husband, she would go back to him. There was no indication that he had changed; he wasn't in therapy for his rage. But now because this woman would not "go back," she was made to drag guilt along with her bruised arms. Forgiveness? Yes—for her own soul's sake—but to tell her she has to return into that nightmare for the sake of God is twisting the truth.

At times we are so interested in maintaining the status quo that we suffocate people under its load. I can hear someone quote Scripture: "But I tell you, Do not resist an evil person. If someone strikes you on the right cheek, turn to him the other also" (Matthew 5:39). It is dangerous to rip a verse out of Scripture and let it stand on its own as the verse for battered women. We need to hear the heart of God.

Husbands, in the same way be considerate as you live with your wives, and treat them with respect as the weaker partner and as heirs with you of the gracious gift of life, so that nothing will hinder your prayers. Finally, all of you, live in harmony with one another; be sympathetic, love as brothers, be compassionate and humble. Do not

*repay evil with evil or insult with insult, but with blessing, because
to this you were called so that you may inherit a blessing.*

1 Peter 3:7–9

As I read this passage about marriage my understanding
of Christ's words in Matthew are fleshed out. We are called
to live above revenge so if someone "slaps" us, we don't repay
that evil by trying to hurt that person in return; we leave our
vindication to the Lord. The woman who is being abused needs
to be taken under the protective wings of friends and the
church—not have guilt added to her bruises.

For those of us who have been hurt by a brother or sister in Christ, trusting God means that we let go of our picture of what "fair" is and rest in God's grace toward us. "May
my vindication come from you; may your eyes see what is right"
(Psalm 17:2).

God's grace enables us to get our glasses cleaned and take
another look around us. As we recognize the humanity of those
who have hurt us and relinquish our desire to get even, we see
broken people whom God loves. This is not easy and it is a
process. I can think that I've forgiven someone, but something will trigger a painful memory and I feel a tidal wave of
old emotions surge over me. I just don't go surfing those emotions anymore! I don't make a day trip out of the feelings. I deal
with them. When I feel those emotions I turn them over to
God before negative *thoughts* rise up to choke me. I ask God to
help and I let go.

Are you saying, "So, it works for you, but not for me. I
can't forgive." Are you sitting there with clenched fists waiting for someone to walk back into the room and apologize?
Well, I think that's probably what happened to Miss Havisham
in *Great Expectations.* Unforgiveness is a trap that is killing only
you—and your joy. You don't have control over anyone else
but yourself, so let go, open the shades, step out into the sun
while you still can.

If you can't "open the shades," then give God permission to open the shades. Commit in your heart that you will

walk in forgiveness, and leave justice up to God. In *What's So Amazing about Grace?* Philip Yancey says, "In the final analysis, forgiveness is an act of faith. By forgiving another, I am trusting that God is a better justice-maker than I am. By forgiving, I release my own right to get even and leave all issues of fairness for God to work out. I leave in God's hands the scales that must balance justice and mercy."

The prophet Habakkuk felt torn apart by the injustice of what was going on around him: "How long, O LORD, must I . . . cry out to you, 'Violence!' but you do not save? Why do you make me look at injustice? Why do you tolerate wrong?" (1:2–3). To him it seemed as if God was doing nothing. But what "seemed" true wasn't. "Then the LORD replied: '. . . the revelation awaits an appointed time; it speaks of the end and will not prove false. Though it linger, wait for it; it will certainly come and will not delay'" (2:2–3). What was the truth? One, no one gets away with anything for ever. Two, God is always doing something. God is at work.

While he's working in others, allow him to work in you, restoring your joy as you relinquish your resentments. Commenting on the forgiveness offered by Joseph to his brothers, Stephen Mitchell, a translator of the stories of Genesis, says forgiveness "is the adult counterpart to the unconscious happiness of childhood where all humans begin. It is a sabbath of the heart."

I HAVE GRACE TO SPREAD THE PEACE

Second Corinthians 5:17–21 is a wonderful passage describing how we are reconciled to God through Christ. In one sense it's a summary of themes in this book, and it draws us beyond ourselves to a ministry of our sharing the Good News with others:

> If anyone is in Christ, he is a new creation; the old has gone, the new has come! All this is from God, who reconciled us to himself through Christ and gave us the ministry of reconciliation: that God was reconciling the world

to himself in Christ, not counting men's sins against them.
And he has committed to us the message of reconciliation.
We are therefore Christ's ambassadors, as though God
were making his appeal through us.

As Christians, whatever our specific ministry might be, we
are called to a "ministry of reconciliation" as "Christ's ambassadors." We're not representing ourselves or our own agenda;
we're representing Christ, and as we represent him we must do
so with humility. Saint Augustine said, "Should you ask me what
is the first thing in religion, I should reply that the first, second, and third thing therein is humility." Yes, some of us are
given jobs that are more public than others, but I've been in
the public eye, and I know—it's a joy not to be a self-appointed
saint. I've learned that Sheila Walsh never has been and never
will be the good news—Jesus is. What a relief! I think Jeremiah
understood this. He spoke for the Lord and yet to the Lord
he said: "When your words came, I ate them; they were my joy
and my heart's delight, for I bear your name, O LORD God
Almighty" (15:16). He knew whom he belonged to and whom
he represented—and knowing that let his heart rest in joy.

In *New Seeds of Contemplation*, Thomas Merton wrote,
"Humility contains in itself the answer to all the great problems of the life of the soul." That's a strong statement! He talks
of "the unquiet world of those who live for themselves."

In 1992 *Discipleship Journal* ran a moving personal story
("A Performance or an Act of Love?") by John Powell, S.J., who
was particularly nervous about a speech he was giving. As the
hour approached he prayed, asking God to take away his anxiety. God didn't respond. John prayed harder. And *then* he
stopped to listen. In his spirit he heard God's answer: "You are
getting ready to give a performance . . . so [your audience] will
know how good you are. . . . I don't want a performance; I want
an act of love." Only then did Powell's anxiety dissipate. As
he saw others as hurting people needing God's love, he walked
into a ministry of reconciliation, allowing God's love to shine
through him.

I don't think I'll ever forget the day a friend called me from out of town. From the tone of her voice I could tell something was terribly wrong. It didn't take long for her to tell me her worry: "I think I'm HIV positive." I listened, struggling to put it all together. I had a picture of a church girl. I had a picture of a prayer partner. I had a picture of a friend whose greatest problem was looking for a new job. Into this picture I tried to fit this new piece of information. I had so many questions, but I knew they would have to wait. "Can you get on to the first flight and come for a few days?" I asked.

"I can be there by five."

As I drove to the airport to pick her up, my mind was reeling. *How? Was she sick now? What made her think she was infected? Had she received a call from someone she had been intimate with? How long would she have to live? If I were in her place, what would I want from a friend? What was I to say and do?*

Well, for starters, we hugged for a long time. We drove around for a while before we went home. We talked about all sorts of moments in our lives—avoiding the real subject at hand as if we were keeping demons at bay by not talking about them. We picked up cappuccinos to go at a trendy new cafe and then we drove to my house. We didn't talk much. I made her some cocoa and showed her the guest room. "I love you," I said as I left her room.

"That's why I'm here," she said.

I couldn't sleep much that night. My heart ached for her. I reflected on the grace and mercy of God to me, and I prayed for her that she would know there was not a grain of sand of judgment in my heart to her. Being broken has a way of cleaning your eye glasses. There is such a freedom and a joy in being released from "fixing" people. There is such a joy in simply loving them. I had no idea what the next few days or months would hold for my friend, but I knew that we would be there together.

The next morning I found a clinic where she could get a blood test. It was set back from the road on a quiet street. Most people didn't even know it was there. It wasn't a place you would go looking for unless you suddenly found yourself needing it.

I parked and we went in. I wondered how many shadowy figures slipped through the heavy doors every day, dragging the weight of the world with them down the drab corridor.

We sat in the waiting room until they called my friend's number. I looked around and then down at my lap, suddenly not wanting to invade the privacy of the others waiting for their numbers to be called. No one spoke. The fluorescent strip light glared down disapprovingly at us. "Number 42." Our number.

"Can my friend come in with me?" my friend asked.

"Yes, that will be fine."

We sat in front of a small wooden desk that might have been rescued from an old school room. The stranger on the other side asked very personal questions that my friend answered quietly without looking into his eyes.

It felt surreal. Our friendship usually took us to noisy bookstores where we drank coffee and laughed together. Now we sat in the bad part of town in a claustrophobically small room, while my friend was being verbally stripped naked by a stranger.

A few days later my friend had to return home. Because she had not yet received the results of her test, she signed a paper authorizing me to pick up her test results. It was a strange responsibility. A lot of people in town knew me. Some people might have said that I was being a stumbling block to others by going to the clinic. What if someone saw me, knew who I was, and put two and two together and came up with nine? But I was her friend. Grace and love have to walk in front of self-preservation, gossip, and superstition.

The Equipping Pastor, coauthored by Paul Stevens and Phil Collins, describes an interesting Old Testament concept: The *shaliach* was a messenger or ambassador sent by a great king to a lesser, vassal king. The *shaliach* had no power or hardly a name in and of himself; he arrived and brought tidings on behalf of the king. If he was received with respect, it meant the great king was received with honor. If he was run out of town, it was received as being an assault against the king—not the *shaliach* himself. Stevens and Collins write, "So it is for those who serve as Christ's ambassadors. They may be well-received or shafted. It does not really matter. They serve God. And their service is not dependent on the acceptance by those to whom they are sent."

To me this means that as ambassadors of Christ we are free to love others and leave the results of our efforts in his hands. I think of an unmarried friend of mine. It used to bother her that no one seemed to notice that she was on her own after church. She would return to her apartment disappointed and alone. Her isolation and subsequent resentment was sapping her joy. Then she heard an interview I did with author Madeleine L'Engle. Madeleine said that often on Sunday mornings she would put a huge casserole in the oven before going to church. Then at church she'd look around and see who seemed to be on their own and maybe she'd notice some friends she hadn't seen for a while—she'd invite them all back to her house for lunch. These spontaneous moments have brought a lot of joy to others and a lot of laughter to her walls.

When my friend heard Madeleine's routine, she decided to give it a try. Once. Of course she was scared. "It always sounds better on television!" she said. *What if nobody comes? What if they'd rather do their laundry than have lunch with me? I'm not a great writer, like Madeleine.* "I was afraid that conversation around my little table would sink like a premature soufflé, but I started anyway."

Once turned into twice and now it is her routine—and her table is the center of joy and reconciliation for any number of people who didn't really want to be doing their laundry on Sunday afternoons.

What if it hadn't worked? If you're an ambassador for Christ, a *shaliach*, the reception you receive isn't something you have to take personally. You're free to share the love of Christ with others—for his sake, for the joy set before you.

I don't know about you, but I've spent too much of my life taking everyone else's temperature to see whether I was all right. But when we are *settled* in our skin, when we are at peace with who we are in Christ, we walk with eyes and hands open. I used to find it very hard to accept criticism. I saw it as a rejection of me as a person rather than of something I was doing. As I have confronted that in my life and have grown into the knowledge of God's stamp of acceptance on my heart, I have become liberated from maintaining my fences as if at any moment I might be destroyed.

I also had an inflated sense of responsibility. For years I wandered around like a demented nurse taking everyone's emotional temperature, but I quit that job. That kind of life is too exhausting. As ambassadors of Christ we are responsible for our actions—before God and toward others. We are called to be reconcilers. But we are not responsible for the actions and reactions of others or for their emotional well-being.

And sometimes that means that people will leave our circle of friends. Sometimes good-byes are inevitable, because you're simply headed in opposite directions. I learned a painful lesson about that a few years ago. A friend was struggling with a passion in her life that was pulling her away from her friendship with God. I was determined not to let go of her but to be there as a constant in her life. My problem came when she wanted to pull me into the same thing. We sat down and I told her that I loved her but that I was not going that way. At first I believed I could hold onto her and keep walking on a straight path. She kept crossing the line. I was frustrated by my inability to tug her with me until I realized that I can't choose the steps of another. How arrogant to imagine that I am powerful enough to will someone else to change her ways. Even Jesus let people walk away.

Three times I sat with my friend for serious heart-to-heart talks. I told her that I loved her, but I knew where I was going and there is no other way home. She never called me again. Perhaps one day when God in his grace touches the heart of my friend and she comes running back to his arms, she'll call me. I hope so. I pray so. I'll be here.

It took me a long time to process this. Was I deserting my friend? Was she deserting me? I would be no friend at all if I watched someone I love stick her hand in a fire and said nothing. But I could not fight the pull of sin in my friend's life. We do the right thing because it's the right thing, and we keep on loving, we keep on hoping, we keep on praying.

Several times I've referred to a key passage in Hebrews 12 that starts with "let us," then walks through shame and joy, and ends in glory: "Let us throw off everything that hinders.... Let us fix our eyes on Jesus, the author and perfecter of our faith, who for the joy set before him endured the cross, scorning its shame, and sat down at the right hand of the throne of God." For the joy set before him—for love—he endured and cast aside any rejection and shame. The writer of Hebrews then turns directly to us readers: "Consider him who endured such opposition from sinful men, so that you will not grow weary and lose heart" (v. 3). Look to Jesus and don't lose heart. Look to Jesus, live as his reconciling ambassador, and learn the truth buried in the book of Proverbs: "There is deceit in the hearts of those who plot evil, but joy for those who promote peace" (12:20).

In chapter 2 I discussed the saboteur of joy—being disappointed with people in the church. My suggestion? If you can't find a church that models the love and truth of Christ, then find the community that is closest to the real thing and go and be that model for them. If you can't find the kind of friend you want, then be that kind of friend to someone. Admit your disappointment—for we are a disappointing bunch. Then forgive and throw yourself in and be what you wish you could find in others. What delight you will bring to the body of Christ! It's impossible to bless others without being blessed yourself. As preacher John Webster said, "It is one of the most beautiful compensations of life that no man can sincerely try to help another without helping himself."

I've had the privilege of meeting with Christians in countries where it still costs very dearly to love God openly. I can't imagine talking to them about self-esteem. They have found themselves—their joy—in their love for God and service to one another. Here in the West we are so affluent and so lonely. We don't feel as if we are needed. Well, you are needed; you just have to jump in. I love Chuck Swindoll's definition of ministry. Just two simple words: *Show up!*

THE OUTWARD WITNESS OF JOY

There's something about joy—it's not contagious, and yet ... genuine joy is a subtle witness that God can multiply like the loaves and fishes. As Jerry Bridges says in *The Practice of Godliness*, "The purpose of rejoicing is not so we can feel better emotionally (though that will happen). The purpose of joy is to glorify God by demonstrating to an unbelieving world that our loving and faithful heavenly Father cares for us and provides for us all that we need."

And a genuine joy can be a witness in ways we don't even realize. In *The Equipping Pastor*, Phil Collins gives a specific example of a *shaliach*—ambassador—who wasn't even aware of how her very life brought joy to others. Phil tells of a hospital call he made on a young woman named Helen who was dying of cancer. When he offered to read Scripture and pray for her, she said, "No, thank you, I have my own religious faith."

But as Phil was leaving, Helen's elderly roommate called him aside and said, "I want to pray for you."

Doing the pastoral thing, Pastor Phil said, "Oh, no I should be praying for you."

"No, you are not going to pray for me today. I am going to pray for you."

Three weeks later he returned—to visit Helen, who was now very close to death. This time she was eager to be prayed for—and eager to tell the pastor of her new faith, which she'd found as a result of her older roommate, who had died. The old woman, Helen said, had been so kind and loving. But Helen was also impressed that she would often sit up in bed and scream with pain. Then she would say, "Praise the Lord. Hallelujah. Praise Jesus."

Was this "ambassador" of Christ (whose name is now forgotten) gritting her teeth and denying her pain? No. She was lifting it up to the Lord, who drew her under his sheltering wing.

Helen continued, "I have come to believe. If that woman, dying in the midst of severe pain, could still praise God, there must be something about her religion. So I asked her about it, and she led me to Christ. I am going to heaven today or someday soon."

The witness of that woman's faith and joy brought young Helen into the kingdom—cause for celebration all around!

In *The Parables of the Kingdom*, Robert Farrar Capon gives his explanation of Jesus' parable that says the kingdom of God is like a treasure found hidden in a field. Someone finding that treasure sells all he has and buys the field "for joy" (Matthew 13:44 KJV). Of course the kingdom of God is not for sale. That's not the point. The point is that it is highly valued treasure. Capon says that buying the field "must be made to stand for nothing less than the ecstatic enjoyment of an utterly precious mystery that would have been cheap at half the price."

Capon proposes that the church "owns" the field in which the treasure is hidden, and we Christians are like sales people who can and should rejoice when someone "buys" the treasure. He says:

> The woman who walks out of Bendel's with a $15,000 mink and the man who pulls into the driveway with a brand-new cream-and-gold Rolls Royce Corniche are not, in that moment at least, gloomy characters. . . . Neither are the salespeople who closed the deals on such fabulous purchases. There is *joy* in heaven over one sinner that repents. . . .
>
> Therefore, there should be at least smiles in the church over the same happy turn of events. . . . because [the customers] have put on the mink of righteousness, sat

down in the Rolls Royce of salvation, and are now just laughing themselves silly over the incongruous wonderfulness of it all.

God gave me a great gift in Boston one summer. I was singing at an evangelistic crusade, one of a team of singers and speakers brought in during the two-week event. I was then cohost of *The 700 Club* and every now and again someone would say, "Thank you, you helped me." But this "thank you" was different: I was standing at the back of the hall, the evening's meeting over, when a couple walked up to me. I guessed they were in their thirties. "Hello!" I said extending my hand. They looked at each other, and then the woman threw her arms around me. "Thank you, thank you, thank you!" she said. I was a little overwhelmed. It had been a good evening, but their response seemed greater than that. "You tell her!" the woman said to her husband.

I looked at the man as he spoke.

"Two years ago," he began, "I was in a very bad place. We were struggling financially, I'd lost my job, it was a mess. I couldn't see a way out so I decided to make one. I decided to take my life. I checked into a cheap motel and I had a gun. I was so desperate. I turned on the television and there you were. I hated Christian TV, but you said that God loved me. You told me that no matter how far away I felt, God loved me. I prayed with you, and I gave my life to God that night."

I was the one who stood with tears running down my cheeks as he talked. What a privilege! Can you imagine the joy in heaven that night? I can tell you there was joy in Boston! When all is said and done, it doesn't get any better than this. We have the joy of sharing the life and light of Christ with others.

You love me Lord, teach me to love.
You fill me Lord, teach me to give.
You are my joy, my heart, my vision.
You are my life, sweet breath of heaven.
Pour through me celestial leaven,

Bread for the hungry, life for the living.
Amen.

GETTING TO JOY

1. Ask the Holy Spirit to bring to mind anyone you have held a grudge against. Write down those names. Take another look at each of these people. Put each in the context of the rest of his or her life. Ask God to help you see this person as a man or woman whom God loves and for whom Christ died. Draw a picture of the one you find hardest to forgive. Pray faithfully for that person for a month and then draw a new picture. Are the two pictures different? How?

2. Write a letter to one person you "cannot" forgive. Pour your heart and anger out on paper. *This letter is for you.* It's not to be mailed or read by anyone else—just you and God. He already knows how you feel and sees what is corroding your inner being. Write till you are exhausted. Write till there is nothing else to say. Then take this letter before the Lord and pray: "Lord, I bring my anger and my unforgiveness to you. I ask you to forgive me for holding on to this, and I open my heart to receive the grace to let it go. In Jesus' name I forgive [name]. Thank you, Lord, for forgiving me. I trust you. Help me to trust you more. Amen."

3. Find a new way to show love where it would come as a surprise. Perhaps you've had a disagreement with a friend or someone in your family and all is not well in your relationship. Do something fun for this person. Bake a cake or buy her a book or a CD that she would enjoy. Soak the discord in grace.

4. Take your joy to a new community. It could be a hospice or a children's hospital or a prison. We live such sheltered lives as Christians clutching God's grace and goodness among ourselves. Take God's love out there where there is little joy and little mercy. As I sat in that dingy clinic that morning with my friend, I felt a strange affinity with

a room full of strangers waiting for a "you live or you die" verdict. Christ is with the broken. He might enjoy some company.

5. Sometimes it's harder to love parents—whom we may want to blame for their contribution to our negative, shameful feelings—than it is to love strangers. If this is problem for you, I suggest you take a new tack: Date your mother. Let me explain what I mean. When you first pursue a new relationship, you give it all you have. You ask questions because you are hungry to know more about this person. You listen, and as trust grows, you share your own hopes and dreams.

Think about your mother. She had a life before you came along. But often we know little about that young woman—her hopes and dreams. Try to draw out that woman. Get to know your mother in ways you haven't before. Celebrate the woman she is. Say thank you. Send flowers. Write her a note. Take her out to dinner. Buy her something she wanted as a child and never got. Move a little closer. Take another picture of her—and replace the old one that wears down your heart.

CHAPTER 10

THE UPWARD PULL OF GRATITUDE

The LORD has done great things for us, and we are filled with joy.

Psalm 126:3

Where there is reason for gratitude, there can always be found a reason for bitterness.

Henri Nouwen, *Life of the Beloved*

L et me return to the story about my friend who thought she might be HIV positive. Because she had to return home, she got permission for me to pick up her test results. So I drove back to the clinic one morning and again sat in the waiting room listening for someone to announce "our" number. There was a palpable tension in the room as we all waited to hear our various verdicts, as we watched the door that led into the inner offices.

Suddenly a young man burst through those doors, joy and relief splashed all over his face. He didn't need to say a word. We all knew that he had been given another chance. He nearly ran out of the clinic, as if to push its memory from his life.

I smiled and said a prayer—that he wouldn't squander his second chance.

In just a minute my number was called. I walked into the inner office as if it were my life that hung in the balance. "The test came back negative," the man behind the desk said. "They run the test several times so there is no mistake."

Now it was my turn to bolt out of that clinic, looking for a phone. As I headed through the waiting room, that relieved young man burst back through the doors, walked up to the receptionist, threw his arms around her, and said, "Thank you!"

The memory of that sight draws me back two thousand years, to a gospel account of Jesus' healing ten leprous men. "One of them, when he saw he was healed, came back, praising God in a loud voice. He threw himself at Jesus' feet and thanked him" (Luke 17:15–16).

Thank you! Just two words. Two powerful words that can change the life of the one who offers them and the one who receives them.

"Thank you" says that we recognize the limits of our own lives.

"Thank you" says that we noticed.

"Thank you" says that our lives have been touched by another and we don't take it for granted.

CHOOSING GRATITUDE

The other night I was driving home with a trunk full of groceries, and I was listening to the local Christian talk station. A Doctor Yusef was speaking, telling a story of a young man determined to humiliate the wise man of the village, the one to whom everyone turned for advice. The younger man caught a bird in his hands and in front of many people asked the old man a question. "Is the bird in my hands dead or alive?"

His trap was easy to see. If the old man said the bird was dead, he would release it and allow it to fly away. If the old man said the bird was alive, he would quickly wring its neck and present a lifeless form. The old man looked at him soberly for a few moments and replied, "It's up to you."

It's up to you. That's the way it is with gratitude.

The only person in this world whom you have any control over is yourself. You can't control your husband, your grown children, your pastor, or your friends, but you can control how you act and respond to situations. I am working hard to bury this truth deep in my heart and in my behavior. My goal is to loosen my grip on the small stuff and tighten my grip on God, and gratitude is key. Let's take a recent example:

I admit, I sometimes get irritated because I feel that Barry doesn't listen to me—like when we were in a hotel, getting ready to go to the first session of a Women of Faith event. It was midafternoon and we hadn't had any lunch. Barry suggested that I take a shower and get ready, and he would walk to a deli and get us something to eat. What did I want? A chicken or tuna sandwich with no mayo.

"Did you get that?" I asked. "No mayo please."

"Yep, I got it," he replied as he walked out the door. "That was *nooooo* mayo."

When he got back I sat down to have my belated lunch. I picked up the sandwich and there it was, mayo, lots of mayo. Barry was innocently eating his burger, and I opened the sandwich in front of him. "What does that look like to you?" I asked.

"Looks like a chicken sandwich," he said nonchalantly.

"No, I mean that gooey stuff all over it," I said, poking at it with a fork as if it were something we'd scraped off our windshield.

"Looks like mayo to me," he replied.

"I told you that I didn't want mayo," I shot back.

"Did you?" he said. "I'm sorry!"

I was so tired and mad that I moved into a tirade of "you never listen, you care only about stuff that matters to you." For at least an hour there was tension between us, until I asked him to forgive me.

Later that evening I was greeting people at my book table. A woman about my age hugged me and said, "It's lovely to see how much you and Barry love each other. Treasure one another!" Then she walked away with tears in her eyes.

I heard the next woman in line quietly say, "She lost her husband last month."

"Excuse me?" I said.

"Just last month her husband died of a heart attack," she continued. "They'd been married only two years."

I prayed for her as Barry and I drove back to the hotel that night. And I looked at Barry with new eyes as the street lights caught the highlights in his blond hair. I wondered how I would feel if the last thing I got to say to him was that he blew my sandwich order.

It's true that Barry doesn't always listen. But when I look at him in gratitude, I see a kind and wonderful man who loves me deeply and is trying hard to be a better listener. He is also a very forgiving man who extends grace when his wife loses it over a jar of Miracle Whip.

So much of the gift and presence of joy has to do with how we choose to live each moment of each day. If you knew that today was the last day you would get to live with those you love, how would it change this day? When Barry leaves his good suit lying in a crumpled heap on the floor, I remind myself that the woman who hugged me that night would probably give her right arm to have her husband's suit lying in a heap on her bedroom floor because they had so little time together. Joy has to do with a daily choice to let the little things go and celebrate the bigger picture—with gratitude.

I propose that ultimately gratitude transforms discontent, that gratitude draws us up and out of our self-absorption— toward joy—as surely as gravity physically pulls us downward.

GRATITUDE GUARDS

Ruth Graham exemplifies for me the grace and wisdom of a godly woman. One evening I sat with her in her home in front of the fireplace, fascinated as the light from the fire danced across her high cheekbones. I was so grateful to be in her presence. We talked for a long time about books we loved and writers we admired. As the fire announced the last dance, Ruth showed me to the guest room. I lay awake for a while, the crisp white sheets pulled up under my chin, and allowed our conversation to wash over me.

"I almost missed that part of the verse," she had said. "But it's the key!"

I reached over to the night stand for my Bible and looked up Philippians 4:6–7: "Do not be anxious about anything, but in everything, by prayer and petition, with thanksgiving, present your requests to God. And the peace of God, which transcends all understanding, will guard your hearts and your minds in Christ Jesus."

What had she "almost missed"? The "with thanksgiving." With thanksgiving!

She'd been telling me about the younger years of her son Franklin, the family rebel. Ruth told me of the nights that she would get down beside her bed and plead for him—the one who walked away from his father's invitations to receive Christ. Her mother's heart was broken. She begged God to "arrest" her son and speak to him. The burden weighed heavily on her soul. Then one night she read again these verses in Philippians. This time she was gifted with new eyes. "With thanksgiving"! That was what was missing from her prayers. From that night onward as she prayed for Franklin, she did it with a grateful heart, thanking God for his life.

It turned her around. It changed everything. It took the burden off her as a mother and tucked it into God's pocket with a "thank you!" It changed the focus from what seemed to be happening and onto a God who works behind the scenes. It allowed the peace of God room to reign in her heart.

In *The Trauma of Transparency*, J. Grant Howard says, "The opportunity to tell [God] everything tends to move us toward unloading on Him all the negative things in our lives. He wants that, but He also wants to hear from us on the positive side too.

"Thanksgiving, adoration and praise are, by their very nature, positive. They cause us to focus on God—who He is, what He has done, what He is doing, and what He can do. This helps us to resist our inevitable tendency to focus on ourselves."

Now, as a man in his forties, Franklin Graham is president of Samaritan's Purse, a Christian relief agency bringing help and hope to the poorest of the poor. I work with him from time to time. I see a man God is raising up in a remarkable way to communicate his love and mercy to a bruised and skeptical world. When I see him, or even think of him, I remember Ruth and I remember God, and I lift my burdens to heaven with a prayer of thanksgiving.

With thanksgiving! With thanksgiving!

Just a few verses after the passage that Ruth illuminated for me, Paul says, "I know what it is to be in need, and I know what it is to have plenty. I have learned the secret of being content in any and every situation, whether well fed or hungry, whether living in plenty or in want" (Philippians 4:12). The word *content* used here in the original Greek text also means "satisfied" or "sufficient." Paul was saying, "I understand now that this is enough, this is all I need." (It's the same word translated as *sufficient* in 2 Corinthians 12:9: "My [God's] grace is sufficient for you.")

Being content—Paul *learned* the secret, apparently it didn't "come naturally." As Mayo Mathers says in an article in *Today's Christian Woman*, "Godly contentment is achievable, depending on which mental list I dwell on—what God *hasn't* done, or what he *has* done."

GRATEFUL TO GOD

Some days "thank you" may seem to be a head-in-the-sand platitude offered out of compulsion rather than authenticity. But I believe it's the most authentic thing we *can* say. I believe that because of who it is we are thanking. We are not asked to stake our life savings on a broken down three-legged horse whose heart may see the finish line but whose body never will. This is God we are talking about! The great and good I AM.

One of my single friends, Katie, has learned to thank God for what he *has* done—and with a bit of humor: "I love God because he's nothing like the guys I date," she says. Then she explains further: "He pursued me. He pursued relationship with me and he followed through. He nurtures me. He keeps his word. He returns all my calls! More than that, when I call he's always there."

She continues, "With God I have found the joy of belonging at last. I feel held onto. I still ache at times, because I'd love to have kids and I'd love to be loved by someone in cowboy boots and blue jeans, but I'm content."

I told Katie about an article I had read in *Discipleship Journal*, an interview with Helene Ashker on contentment. Ashker told of a seminar in which participants were challenged to thank God for the thing they hated in their lives—which for her meant her singleness. In the interview she said, "Thanking the Lord for my singleness was a totally absurd idea to me." But she began to do it, and she continued: "It was probably at least a year later when it dawned on me that the ache about being single had disappeared."

Katie said she could understand that—and so did my friend Claire, a woman in her fifties who's been a widow for about two years. "After months of grief and tears and anger at God, I found a new place in him. As a young woman I had a vibrant, passionate relationship with Jesus, but when I met Sam I transferred a lot of my love to him. It was his shoulder I leaned on. It was Sam I asked to help me when I couldn't see my way out of the trees. Now that I've regained some of my balance again I have a new appreciation for life, for every moment. I have a thankful heart. I guess that's what contentment is to me. I'd love to marry again, but if I don't, I believe I'll be content."

Is "being widowed" what she would have chosen for this season of her life? "No! I would never have chosen this." As she says that her eyes fill with tears. "All I'm saying is that in the greatest despair of my life when I was lying in the dust, a tree grew up over me and sheltered me"—the sheltering, shading tree of a faithful, loving God.

PURE JOY?

In an earlier chapter I told of discovering James 1:5—a prayer instruction that starts, "If any of you lacks wisdom, he should ask God, who gives generously to all without finding fault." Now every day—with thanksgiving—I pray for wisdom: "Show me what to do, and I will do it with all my heart. . . . When you close a door—even a door I wish would open—I will thank you." I live by this prayer. Recently I had what I perceived to be a very important business lunch. My expected outcome was that the man I was meeting would represent me and oversee our business office. As I drove to my appointment I prayed the "wisdom" prayer. But then as I wrestled with my pasta, this guy told me that he felt that it was the wrong time for him to be involved with my husband and me. After lunch I drove away with tears running down my face. They were not tears of disappointment. They were tears of gratitude. My heavenly Father said, "This isn't the best thing." And I said, "Thank you!" Even when it doesn't make sense to me, I'm learning to trust God.

But sometimes I admit that "the plan"—God's plan—isn't quite as easy to see or be grateful for. James must have realized this, as the "ask for wisdom" sentence is preceded by a "difficult" description of "pure joy." "Consider it pure joy, my brothers, whenever you face trials of many kinds, because you know that the testing of your faith develops perseverance. Perseverance must finish its work so that you may be mature and complete, not lacking anything" (James 1:2–4).

What? Testing? Perseverance? Pure joy?

Yes—it's a "pure joy" that looks forward to the "complete work" that Paul also mentions: "He who began a good work in you will carry it on to completion until the day of Christ Jesus" (Philippians 1:6). My friend Steve Lorenz has taught me to value and understand the importance of *process*, which the dictionary defines as "a series of actions, changes, or functions bringing about a result." God is at work in all of life if we will only see his hand and listen and learn. God is talking to us all the time. We imagine that if good things happen, then God loves us, and if life seems difficult, then he doesn't. This isn't true. Join hands with God in your life. Throw open the doors and let the sun come pouring in. God is at work! God is at work! God is at work!

It's a "pure joy" that knows one's past is covered by the God who is love; one's present is enveloped by the God who is faithful; one's future is hidden in the hands of the God of hope. Romans 15:13 indicates that there's an "upward spiral" of hope—that leads to joy—that leads to hope. "May the God of hope fill you with all joy and peace as you trust in him, so that you may overflow with hope by the power of the Holy Spirit." I talk to my friend Alice on the phone as she battles with brain cancer. I listen as she moans; I listen as her husband, Roger, tries to comfort her. I tell them both it's going to be all right. What do I mean? I don't know *how* God makes things all right; I just know that ultimately he does. Sometimes he reaches out a finger from heaven and in a moment the most hopeless situation is infused with light and life. Sometimes it's as if God closes the book and there is nothing more to say. I don't always understand everything with my mind, but in my spirit I know without a shadow of doubt that God is here, God is still on the throne; it's going to be all right!

It's a pure joy that learns to take one day—one hour—at a time. Author Christopher de Vinck had a brother who was unable even to get out of bed for the thirty-two years of his life. Christopher tells how his parents patiently fed him, spoonful by spoonful, every bite he ate. Christopher once asked his father how they maintained their positive can-do attitude, and his dad explained that he asked himself one question: "Can I feed Oliver today?" *Yes, I can feed him today—and tomorrow? I will face tomorrow when it comes. And tomorrow, God will be faithful and will give me grace and strength enough.*

That is something to be grateful for. That is reason to celebrate.

BRING BACK MY JOY?

Perhaps you look at your life at the moment and, although your head agrees with everything I've said, your heart says, "I just can't do it!" Let Paul's words wash over you. "My [God's] grace is sufficient for you, for my power is made perfect in weakness" (2 Corinthians 12:9). You're right! You can't do it. I can't do it either. We don't have to.

Remember how closely related the Greek words are for grace and joy: *charis* and *chara*. God's grace shows up to plug our leaky lives. That's the gospel. That's the good news.

Do you *really want* to find the joy? Then reach out. Throw yourself at God's mercy. Ask him to show you his love. Give him some room to move in. After one recent conference I spent a long time talking to a woman. She *couldn't* believe that God loved her. We talked on and on. I opened my Bible and showed her verse after verse about the love of God, to no avail. I suddenly realized that she *wouldn't* believe that God loved her. The gift is yours. Ask God here and now to allow you a glimpse of his love.

When asked about a breakthrough of the heart—"But how can God bring this about in me?"—George MacDonald said, "Let him do it, and perhaps you will know."

Let God love you, and even before you "feel" the warmth, start walking a thank-you journey.

> *What joy!*
> *Our joy!*
> *Throw your hands up in the air and dance in the grass.*
> *Laugh like a baby and cry like a saint.*
> *Then fall on your knees and worship.*
> *Life is good!*
> *God is good!*
> *Joy to the world!*

GETTING TO JOY

1. In her book *A Time for Risking*, Miriam Adeney proposes
   writing a personal prayer centered on the repeating phrase
   of a psalm, such as "His mercies endure forever."

   I decided to focus on the phrase "God is faithful" and
   to pray it in light of my day.

   > *Christian slept till 7:00 A.M.:*
   >   *God is faithful. . . .*
   > *Ian got his job:*
   >   *God is faithful. . . .*
   > *The pipes have burst under the house, and we'll need a*
   >   *new floor in the kitchen:*
   >   *God is faithful. . . .*
   > *Aunt Mary came through her surgery:*
   >   *God is faithful. . . .*

   Why not buy a journal and write a prayer like this at
   the end of each day? What a wonderful record of the mercies and faithfulness of God.

2. Try this prayer and "inventory," as described by John Ackerman in *Spiritual Awakening*, who quotes a friend (active
   in Alcoholics Anonymous) describing his daily practice:
   "First, I think over the day and thank God for the good stuff.
   Then I think if there was any bad stuff. If it's my fault, I
   make amends first thing in the morning if I can. If I'm sore
   about the way someone else treated me, I take it up with
   them right away. Then I pray for my family and people I
   work with and lie down and sleep." I love this practice of
   doing your spiritual laundry every day rather than letting it
   pile up in the corner waiting for Sunday. How liberating to
   start every new day with clean sheets!

3. Keep a gratitude journal. In *Simple Abundance*, Sarah Breath-
   nach suggests keeping a journal at our bedside and every
   night before turning off the light writing down five things

we are thankful for in that day. I like that. On tough days it would do our hearts good to pick it up and see page after page of the kindness of God. And when we think we have nothing to be thankful for, the exercise of bringing what's true about God's goodness to us before our eyes will put a dent in any dispirited day.

We can thank God for our husbands or children, for our friends and our health. We can thank him for a waggy-tailed dog welcoming us home from a thankless day at work. We can thank him for two eyes that see or the ears to listen to music that soothes our souls or moves our feet. It's up to us! Write it down and remember the goodness of God and the joy of life.

4. Grace in an envelope. When I was a little girl I was introduced to the world of thank-you notes. The day after Christmas was about turkey sandwiches, trips to the store for batteries, and letters to aunts and uncles to thank them for an odd assortment of gifts from hand-knitted hats to Avon perfume. I have maintained that habit and extended it. I don't particularly like letter writing. I get antsy, I'd much rather pick up the phone. But I like what it does. I have a few friends I have never met whom I know well through the mail. Some of them are viewers who used to watch me on *The 700 Club* or people who were touched by something I wrote in a book. I have a list and I write to them regularly. Each time I thank them for something in their lives or letters that I appreciate. The world is full of lonely people who haven't heard "thank you" in a long time. Ask God to bring someone to your mind and sit down and send a little grace in an envelope.

5. The habit of gratitude. Look for opportunities to thank the "familiar" people in your life. Notice when they do something kind or thoughtful. It's easy to take our families, friends, and coworkers for granted. They are *supposed* to act that way if they love us. That may be true, but what a wonderful gift

when those who are as familiar to us as our own faces stop, take hold of us, look into our eyes, and say, "Thank you!"

6. Choose to meditate on these Scriptures:

Enter his gates with thanksgiving and his courts with praise; give thanks *to him and praise his name. For the* LORD *is good and his love endures forever; his faithfulness continues through all generations.*

Psalm 100:4–5 (emphasis added)

Rejoice in the Lord always. I will say it again: Rejoice!

Philippians 4:4

Let the peace of Christ rule in your hearts, since as members of one body you were called to peace. And be thankful.

Colossians 3:15

Let the word of Christ dwell in you richly as you teach and admonish one another with all wisdom, and as you sing psalms, hymns and spiritual songs with gratitude in your hearts to God.

Colossians 3:16

PART 4

ENHANCING
THE JOY

How good is . . . life . . . how fit to employ
All the heart and soul and the senses for ever in joy!
Robert Browning

Command those who are rich in this present world not to be
arrogant nor to put their hope in wealth, which is so uncertain,
but to put their hope in God, who richly provides us with every-
thing for our enjoyment.
1 Timothy 6:17

ꝺ

The King James Version of the Bible uses *joy* as a verb—
the way we might use *rejoice*. God "will joy over" his people
(Zephaniah 3:17). Paul and his companions "joy for" other
Christians (1 Thessalonians 3:9). I like it! And that's how I'm
using *joy* in the chapter titles in this section.

As we allow God to restore our internal joy, we can
enhance that delight by looking for ways to joy in and celebrate
God's goodness and creation. In 1 Timothy 6:17, Paul says God
"richly provides us with everything for our enjoyment." And
the older I get the more I realize that life is a chatter box if
you listen. (Being a mother has sharpened my hearing. My
life has become a parable that unfolds before me every day
through a little bundle in diapers.) God is all around us speaking volumes if our hearts are open to hear the ways in which he
can speak to us, enhancing our joy.

CHAPTER 11

JOY IN MAKING MUSIC

Flowers appear on the earth; the season of singing has come, the cooing of doves is heard in our land.

Song of Songs 2:12

True religion sings here, and will sing more hereafter. Distrust your religion unless it is cheerful, unless it turns every act and deed to music, and exults in attempts to catch the harmony of the new life.

Phillips Brooks

I sang my final concert of 1996 two days before Christian was born. I'd promised a church in San Juan Capistrano that I would do a Christmas concert. I was *very pregnant*. I felt like a show-and-tell exhibit as I sang of Mary's journey to Bethlehem and hoped my hosts had more than a donkey to get me out of there fast if I needed to. It was hard to catch my breath that evening, but I was doing fairly well until I came to "Silent Night," at which point Christian woke up in my womb and began to dance to the song. Have you ever tried to sing with a squirrel up your sweater?

Does he know that music has been a part of his world since before he was born? He's now eleven months old. I watch him express himself. He can't say many words. There's "da da" and "ba ba," and on a good day he'll throw in "ma ma," but he has a lot more to say—so he sings. Now, it's nothing he'll get a record contract for, but it serves him when he's so happy he could burst because he doesn't have the right words to say. We'll be standing in line at the grocery store and he'll burst into . . . something, at the top of his voice. Part of it seems to be his way of getting out what's inside and part of it seems to be throwing a cord to Barry and me and others—communication, shared joy.

Believe me, I love making music—singing my heart out. Since childhood music has been a solace to me—comforting me when I was down, drawing my body, soul, and spirit into a realm beyond the walls of my own self.

Making music gives us renewed vision or passion; it tells us we're still alive. I remember walking down the long white corridor of the psychiatric hospital after I had been there for two weeks. I suddenly stopped, amazed by what I was hearing. I was singing. It was only when I heard myself that I realized I hadn't sung for a long time. That was when I knew that I was going to be all right.

In a *Charisma* article, "Music's Mysterious Power" (February 1986), John Michael Talbot says making music is powerful because it "involves both mind and heart." Talbot is talking primarily of Christian music, but this is true of making music, period. Have you ever watched a jazz sax player pouring out his heart—and lungs—playing the blues?

You may be familiar with Karaoke video and sound programs. Taped musicians play "back up" for familiar popular tunes, while the song lyrics are highlighted word by word on a video screen—so you, the viewer, can sing along (preferably with a mike in hand and preferably in front of a partying audience). For a moment you are Elton John or Bette Midler. On a cruise ship recently, Barry and I decided to check this out. Maybe it was because we were in the company of relative strangers whom we might never see again, maybe it was just the holiday spirit, but people were freed up in unusual ways. One after another they took the mike and belted out their songs. Finally Barry couldn't sit still any longer. He delivered a heartfelt version of "Rhinestone Cowboy." Some of the renditions were downright painful to hear, but it was interesting to watch what was happening among us. We clapped as loudly for those whose voices would have made a dog's ears bleed as we did for those who could give some pop singers a run for their money.

One singer stood out to me. A doctor confined to a wheelchair took the mike, and for those moments her soul had wings that transported her where her legs would not. I saw the joy in her face, in her eyes, a lightness that came to her. The making of music took her beyond herself.

In a *Christianity Today* article, "Chords That Bind" (September 1, 1997), Philip Yancey tells of his college days when his life was a cauldron of confusion. But for an hour every night he found peace, sitting at a piano, playing classical music. "My own fingers pressed a tactile order onto the world . . . here I sensed a hidden world of beauty, light as a cloud and startling as a butterfly wing. I was experiencing common grace perhaps consciously for the first time, through music."

In *Imagination: Embracing a Theology of Wonder*, Cheryl Forbes tells of a woman named Susan who intentionally set out to heighten her own and her family's imagination. Among other things, she took piano lessons, as she had as a child. For half an hour a day she played Mozart or Chopin or running scales. "To think about what the composer had heard when he wrote a particular sonata or mazurka, to have the rhythms and harmonies extend from the imagination through fingers and onto the keyboard, and to venture her own interpretations regardless of the editor's markings, simultaneously exhilarated and relaxed Susan." She even saw the good effect her practice had on her children, as they saw her "practice diligently, make mistakes without tantrums, work slowly and patiently to get a phrase just right. They began to practice [music lessons] with a different attitude; she watched them approach difficult school work with less fuss or tears."

If you've always wished you had taken piano lessons, it's not too late. We just bought a piano, and one of my goals for the new year is to take lessons. Becoming perfect is not the point; enjoying the process is.

We all have our own ways of making music. Stop for a moment and think. What do you do? Do you whistle or hum, drum your fingers on the desk to a melody in your head? It's part of us, like Ahab in *Moby Dick* by Herman Melville. "While the mate was getting the hammer, Ahab without speaking was slowly rubbing the gold piece against the skirts of his jacket, as if to heighten its luster, and without using any words was meanwhile lowly humming to himself, producing a sound so strangely muffled and inarticulate that it seemed the mechanical humming of the wheels of his vitality in him."

A traditional Quaker song asks a question at the core of the joyful life:

> *My life flows on in endless song, above earth's lamentation; . . .*
> *It sounds an echo in my soul; how can I keep from singing?*

Maybe your joyful question is "How can I keep from humming?" Or "How can I keep from dancing?" In *Stretching the Soul*, Ron Wilson talks about his years of widowhood and how learning to dance helped heal his grief. "If we let the flesh rule while we dance, it can be little more than lust. If we seek simply to satisfy our own fancy and follow our own aspirations, the dance degenerates into a meaningless set of motions. But walk through life with an awareness of the Spirit, and we can express the highest degree of ecstasy in God by moving our feet, arms, and body." It's as if the body is making music with the music.

John Michael Talbot said that to make "real music," "a spark has to come from somewhere deep inside the musician's heart to provide the final ingredient that makes music."

Talbot uses a metaphor to describe Christian music, which draws us to God. "Music is like a kiss between husband and wife. A kiss symbolizes the love of marriage, but it also stirs up that love and leaves it stronger."

We can make music in any number of ways, but I'm especially partial to singing. Augustine said, "He who sings prays twice."

The biblical saints seemed to understand this. When God brought Moses and the children of Israel safely across the Red Sea, they sang: "I will sing to the LORD, for he is highly exalted. The horse and its rider he has hurled into the sea. The LORD is my strength and my song; he has become my salvation. He is my God, and I will praise him, my father's God, and I will exalt him" (Exodus 15:1–2). That's Israel's very first poem—and it's a song to their Lord. In *The Cloister Walk*, Kathleen Norris notes that in the Old Testament "the command that Israel receives most often is to sing."

The last words of King David were not about his strength as a warrior or power as a leader, but about the gift of music. In his last words, David identified himself as "the man exalted by the Most High, Israel's singer of songs" (2 Samuel 23:1).

When Paul and Silas were beaten till every part of their body ached, they sang—in prison, their feet shackled. "About midnight Paul and Silas were praying and singing hymns to God, and the other prisoners were listening to them" (Acts 16:25).

Music is a language we all embrace and all understand. You can say in three minutes of a song what it would take an hour to try and communicate any other way. We feel safe with music and we let our guards down. We identify with the joy or sorrow expressed by the words and the melody melded together in one sound package.

The wonderful thing about *singing* music is that you don't have to be good at it to receive comfort and joy and strength from it. For fun, for long walks in the woods, in the shower—we can all be Aretha Franklin.

On our recent cruise our ship was docked one evening in Bermuda. The members of our "Christian party" enjoyed a candlelight communion service at St. Peter's Church. A few of us—the "professionals"—who were hosting this group stood

at the front of the church leading the singing. I became aware
of a distinctive sound coming from halfway down the pews. I
saw it was Mary, a missionary with cerebral palsy who also suf-
fers terribly handicapping arthritis. Her walk is affected, as is
her speech. She has to commit to communicate; it's even harder
for her to make herself understood. But she stood that evening
in the candle glow, singing her heart out to God. I stopped
singing and listened to her. I stopped singing and watched her.
Her face shone. Tears ran down her cheeks as she sang of her
love for Christ and as he met her in the sacrifice of singing. I
could hear God saying *what a beautiful sound.* He was joying
in her song!

One of the many things I love about my friend Joni
Eareckson Tada is her commitment to singing. We've sung
hymns together in her van on the way to lunch, at a meeting
with our publisher. Everywhere you go with Joni, you notice
that she sings, and every time I'm with her I feel better for being
there. What is it about singing that lifts our spirits?

There is something spiritual about singing, something
mystical. In *The Cloister Walk*, Kathleen Norris recounts the
story of a young evangelical girl raped and murdered during
a massacre of peasants in El Salvador in 1981. Years later the
murderers were interviewed and haunted by what they had seen
and heard. The girl wouldn't stop singing her songs of faith.
Throughout a whole afternoon they brutalized her, and she
kept singing. They shot her in the chest, and she kept singing,
quieter but the hymns kept flowing, along with the blood. They
shot her again. Surely she was dead, but she kept singing—so
faithfully that the soldiers were spooked—afraid of the phe-
nomenon. Finally, when they took machetes to her neck, the
singing stopped.

At least that's what the soldiers thought. But I don't think
it really did. When the songs of faith, hope, and love are that
much a part of who we are, we will never stop singing. Music
is the one gift of earth that is a gift of heaven. That child kept
right on singing—in the presence of her Lord and Song.

I want to encourage you to make music. Sing out your pain. Sing out your petitions. Sing out your praise.

"You've not heard me," you say.

Well, that doesn't matter. It will do your soul good and God's heart good. God delights in the praises of his people, not in the ones with good voices but those with hearts for him. Singing lifts up our heads. It's a promise of days to come.

"The ransomed of the LORD will return. They will enter Zion with singing; everlasting joy will crown their heads. Gladness and joy will overtake them, and sorrow and sighing will flee away" (Isaiah 51:11). Singing is an appetizer of eternity.

GETTING TO JOY

1. Shared music gives us a sense of community and identity. Check your local radio stations. They cater to country fans or music of the seventies, classic rock or golden oldies, everything from Verdi to Vegas. Music can bond Christians together—even if they have little else in common. Invite friends to your home for an evening of singing. Ask if you can borrow hymnbooks from the church, or simply gather in around a piano. Welcome people to bring instruments, such as guitars. Invite them to choose a favorite hymn or song and come ready to tell why it has special meaning to them.

2. Bill and Gloria Gaither have a lovely Christmas Eve tradition. They call it Soup and Carols. Gloria cooks up big pots of soup, and they invite a bunch of friends in to eat the soup and sing around the piano. Perhaps you could take the carol-sing idea and add your own culinary delight.

3. Write a song! Why not? It doesn't have to be "How Great Thou Art." You might pick a tune you love and write your own words to the Lord and use it in your devotions. Sing it often. I think God would love it.

4. When you're having a bad day, try singing. Dig out an old hymnbook or go and buy one. You won't feel like it at first,

but you'll be amazed how it will lift your spirits and bring back joy to your heart. Better yet, have a hymnal with your Bible. As part of your daily quiet time, sing one hymn.

5. "Let the saints ... sing for joy on their beds" (Psalm 149:5). Forget counting sheep. Sing yourself to sleep tonight— maybe with a favorite hymn or praise song, maybe with a childhood lullaby.

6. If you once played a musical instrument, pick it up and try making a joyful noise. If you don't have an instrument, rent one for one week or a month—just to see if it gives you a bit of pleasure. (If a piano is out of the question, rent a small electronic keyboard.) If there's any spark, sign up for a few months of lessons.

7. Ask for a tambourine for Christmas or your birthday.

8. For one day, sing your table graces—make up a tune. Or sing (chant) a morning blessing on your day (in the car or as you put on your makeup).

CHAPTER 12

JOY IN LISTENING
TO MUSIC

*David would take his harp and play. Then relief would come to
Saul; he would feel better, and the evil spirit would leave him.*
1 Samuel 16:23

Music ... is no invention of ours; it is the gift of God.
Martin Luther

❧

Some of my favorite concerts now take place in a white rocking chair in Christian's bedroom. He'll reach up and touch
my face or lie back and listen. Sometimes he'll burst out laughing, which can be a little disconcerting if I'm halfway through
"Jesus Loves Me This I Know." But he should laugh with
delight. Martin Luther said, "The devil does not stay where
music is."

I remember the first time I heard Handel's *Messiah*. My
mom took Frances and me to hear a local choral society's presentation of this inspired work. The music is beautiful, but one
moment stood out for me in particular. The soprano soloist
took the stage, and as she sang "I know that my Redeemer
liveth," I wept for joy. Not only was the music moving; the message was real. I could have stood up and cheered, but I had a
feeling that the Kilmarnock Choral Society would have frowned
on that!

From ancient days music has been appreciated for its healing effects. When King Saul was tormented almost out of his mind, David's harp playing would quiet his spirit. The book *Cancer Nursing* notes that music therapy can reduce the nausea and bring calm to people suffering the effects of chemotherapy. Music is healing. Music therapists working with Alzheimer's patients have had unusual results reaching some who had seemed mentally "departed" from life. Researchers at the University of Alabama conducted a study with ten men and women with dementia and Alzheimer's. Patients who had long been unresponsive sang along when they heard a therapist sing "What a Friend We Have in Jesus" and "Amazing Grace." The familiar, soothing words and melodies drew them out for a brief moment back to the community of "the living." A piece of heaven granted here on earth.

Classical music has a particularly powerful effect, even on unexpected audiences. It was an unlikely match. Pop radio and Gregorian chants. In 1994 a CD named simply "Chant" was released by the Benedictine brothers of the abbey of Santo Domingo de Silos. It went double platinum, selling two million copies in the U.S. alone in seventeen weeks. Was it a sign of spiritual renewal? It seems not. The crest didn't last long. But for a moment it offered a glimpse for many into a new world.

Not all but much of the great classical music was written to the glory of God. Gregorian chant is biblical text set to music. It's singing prayer. And for a few weeks the voices of monks washed over bars and bookstores, soaking unsuspecting souls in praise to God. Doesn't God move in mysterious ways? Too often we keep the grace and voice of God locked within the four walls of our churches, but Christ spilt himself on the masses. And so did the brothers from Santo Domingo de Silos. They poured their souls out to God across the airwaves—and no one said, "This violates my constitutional rights." The Gregorian chants are in Latin. It's hard to be offended when you don't understand the words.

I interviewed Ben Carson, head of pediatric neurosurgery at Johns Hopkins University. He said he listens to classical music as he engages in delicate brain surgery. The music is calming to the soul. A cord to heaven.

Perhaps you have never exposed yourself to the world of classical music. I was fortunate to grow up in a family where classical music, indeed music of all kinds, was prized. I was introduced to Grieg, Mozart, and Tchaikovsky at an early age and loved to listen along as Mom would tell us the stories of the "Hall of the Mountain King" or the dancing swans. We were taught to listen, to hear the different instruments. Maybe you think classical music isn't "your thing"? Give it one more try. Patrick Kavanaugh has written a book that walks you through various classical music pieces—explaining how to listen, what to listen for. It's *Music of the Great Composers*, available from Zondervan. (He's also written *Raising Musical Kids*, for parents concerned about the musical heritage they're leaving the next generation.)

Music is powerful in the way it works on—and helps us work through—our emotions. Music was a gift of grace at the recent funeral of Diana, Princess of Wales. A nation was still in shock, the world had lost a hero, two little boys had lost their mother. In respect, the cameras stayed away from the family during the service, but from someone who attended I heard that Elton John's "Good-bye, England's Rose" drew out the family's grief. That's music. Those boys were so brave through the whole ordeal, greeting the crowds graciously, joining the funeral procession. They held up through all of that, but when Elton sang good-bye, tears flowed.

Perhaps if words are mind to mind, music is soul to soul. And hearing appropriate music draws out that "soul" in us. It draws out our grief. It can draw out our loyalties. (There's an old Scottish proverb that says, "Twelve Highlanders and a bagpipe makes a rebellion." But take the bagpipe away and we'll run for the hills.) It can draw us to God. In her book *A Time for Risking*, Miriam Adeney describes a conversation she had with her father, the son of a pastor. One day she asked him, "Dad, was it your father's preaching that brought you to Christ?" He thought a minute and said no, "I think it was more my mother's singing." I've heard my own mother talk about the powerful effect of my father's singing. He had a wonderful voice. As he would sing songs like "The Ninety and Nine"—about God's love—God would reach out and draw listeners to himself.

One of the greatest gifts I received from my time at the Christian Broadcasting Network came almost five years after I left. While I was still cohost of *The 700 Club*, I wrote a song called "Jennifer," a modern retelling of the Prodigal Son parable, with Jennifer as the wandering daughter. One day I sang the song on the show and then took a few moments to talk to anyone watching who felt far away from God with no way home. The shows go out live, but they are also saved and sometimes rebroadcast at a later date.

I left in '92. In the spring of '97 I got a call from one of the producers encouraging me to watch the show in a few days. "You'll be blown away by what you see," she said. I tuned in, not knowing what to expect—and I saw a woman named Jennifer. She had been a high-class call girl, strung out on cocaine and alcohol, ready to give up on life. She had arrived in Hollywood with the dream of becoming a hairdresser to the stars. Jennifer had moved in with a man with all the right connections, and soon she was hanging out at the Playboy mansion or having her photo taken with Sylvester Stallone, Kirk Douglas, and other "bright lights." Her boyfriend would beat her until someone hearing her screams would send for the police. "Next time we see you, you'll be dead," an officer told her on one particularly violent night when she refused to press charges. She had a broken nose and a punctured artery—and then Jennifer was told she had cancer. "I knew I'd be dead by thirty," she said.

At the bottom of the barrel, now living by herself, one night she was free-basing cocaine with the television on for light. It was tuned to *The 700 Club* and I was singing. She was crying out to God, "If only I knew that you are real. Speak to me, God." At that moment I began to sing "Jennifer, come home, we are waiting for you." She watched, tears pouring down her face, wishing it could be true. Even as she voiced her "It's too late for me. There's no way you could love me, God," I finished singing and said, "Whoever you are, it's not too late for you. God knows where you've been and what you've done and he loves you. He's waiting for you to come home."

Music is powerful in any hands—but in God's it's life changing. Jennifer heard those words, called the number on the screen, and prayed to receive Christ as her Savior. She is now a committed Christian with a whole new life, talking to other girls in trouble on the streets of Hollywood about the joy she has found in Jesus.

In *Spiritual Moments with the Great Hymns*, Evelyn Bence tells the story of Peggy, who was drawn to Christ by hearing Cynthia Clawson sing the soundtrack of *Trip to Bountiful*. "Softly and tenderly, Jesus is calling ... Come home." Peggy says,

> For weeks afterward I sang that song and tried to learn the words. I sang and cried while I did the dishes. I sang and cried while I folded the clothes. One day my husband started singing along. Startled, I asked him how he knew the words. He said it was an old hymn they sang in all the Baptists churches.... I was amazed—right here in my own home was someone who could teach the words to me. "How could you know this song and not sing it or share it?" I demanded.

Peggy had been hungry to hear the music! Maybe you know a song someone else needs to hear. Maybe you know a song you need to hear anew, as if you were hearing it for the first time. Why not invite some friends over for a listening party? Pick out some beautiful music and enjoy it together, be blessed and fed together.

There is music all around. If you live in the country or near a park, stand outside for a while and listen. Take a blanket and lie down on the grass and close your eyes and listen. You may hear birds singing. You may hear locusts humming. You may hear oaks creaking. You may hear God's choir.

When Jesus taught the parable of the sower, he closed by saying, "He who has ears to hear, let him hear" (Mark 4:9). The implication is clear. Some people are going to hear more than others. Some people are tuned into the voice of God and some are not. I hear this message as a warning to stop and listen to the music, to the Word, to others, to the lessons around us every day. Can't you tell when you're with someone who's listening? She hears you, really hears you. He hears the sadness in your tone or catches your joy. Be a listener, to music, to life, to others, to God. Life is noisy, but there is music in every heartbeat. God is waiting to bring joy and peace to the confusion of our days.

Carve out some moments for yourself to be filled with joy and peace, with a fresh sense of wonder and worship through the gift of music.

Then thank God for what you hear.

GETTING TO JOY

1. Spend some time in a music store where you can listen to some selections before you buy. Try something new. Try a new folk singer, a new gospel singer. Pick a classical composer you're not familiar with and let the music flow over you.

2. Set aside listening time every day, even if it's just ten minutes. Put on an album of hymns and let the words grace your soul. Just listen as if it's the first time you've heard the music and the words. Let the music wash through your soul.

3. As you get ready to eat dinner, put on some soothing background music. If you have a family, don't announce what you're doing. Just do it for a week and see if anyone notices; see if it changes the mood of your tabletime. (You might try lighting a candle too.)

4. Take some children to a concert and then take them out for pizza to talk about what they heard. Give them paper and

crayons and ask them to put down in colors what the music said to them.

5. If you have a piano but don't play much, have a party and invite someone who does play. Let that glorious sound vacuum your carpet and dust your drapes!

6. Find out if you can visit a local retirement home or children's hospital and take some music. It could be a few voices or a CD player. Spread a little joy. Let the music heal.

7. In *This World and Beyond*, theologian Rudolf Bultmann said, "It would be a sad day for us if ever the music of church bells were to become silent in our villages." Think about it. Maybe there isn't a church bell in your town or neighborhood. (Maybe there should be.) Next time you hear a church bell—this week or two years from now on vacation—stop and listen to it. Let it invite you to worship God in your heart.

8. Go for a walk—or just step outside the front door—and listen. Listen for music—birds, rustling wind. If what you hear is honking traffic or a rumbling train, listen with ears that transform the noise into music.

CHAPTER 13
JOY IN THE SENSES

Everything God created is good, and nothing is to be rejected if it is received with thanksgiving, because it is consecrated by the word of God and prayer.

1 Timothy 4:4–5

I n a fun book *Creating a SenseSational Home*, Terry Willits says, "In his goodness and creativity, [God] has given us eyes to see, ears to hear, noses to smell, mouths to taste and talk, and bodies to feel. Each sense is a rich blessing that enhances our life in a unique way and can bring immense pleasure or pain. Though every sense is wonderful, we seldom encounter only one at a time. Instead, God has intricately wired them together to allow us to experience all dimensions of life as we take in the world around us."

She continues, "The role of the senses in memory is so strong that many memories in life are often simply recollections of our stimulated senses."

Whenever I smell a Casablanca lily, it reminds me of my wedding in Charleston, South Carolina. All sorts of images come back to me. The sound of the majestic pipe organ in St. Matthew's Church, the sight of the two darling little flower girls who wore white dresses and carried a garland of lilies between them, the purple of my mother's hat, the haunting melody of the bagpipes as they played her down the aisle, the sparkling of the Christmas tree lights in the reception hall.

It's so easy to walk through life hardly aware of the delight that is ours if we just allowed ourselves to be aware of the moment—the small graces that God sprinkles along our way, like red rose petals strewn before a bride. Ruth Vaughn proposes that little graces we receive through our senses are *Letters Dropt from God.*

George Fox, one of the founding Quakers, thought that a vital relationship with God heightened his senses. Journal entries at the time of his conversion say that he perceived "all things" to be new. "And all the creation gave unto me another smell than before, beyond what words can utter." When he found the joy of the Lord, he thought his world smelled better!

I think maybe there is an upward spiral that exists between our senses and our awareness of God: God can heighten our senses and our senses can heighten our awareness of God. Terry Willits proposes that God has given us our senses primarily "so that we would stand in awe of him and be grateful for his goodness to us."

Let's take a brief look at the delights of three sense: sight, taste, and scent.

JOY IN VISUAL BEAUTY

It was your own eyes that saw all these great things the LORD has done.

Deuteronomy 11:7

In *Behold the Glory*, Chad Walsh said that he usually walked across the college campus where he taught without much noticing anything out of the ordinary. But then, occasionally, "I have suddenly caught myself seeing it with new eyes, as though I were a visitor from another planet. The very trees take on the individuality of loved faces....

"And the paths. For a short while I see paths as they really are—the veins and arteries of social and intellectual relations between one human being and another."

I was driving down a familiar road in Nashville one fall day when I almost drove off the road, the beauty was so intense.

It was a road that I was used to taking, but it looked as if God had sent in a team of the world's finest artists overnight—and I was privy to the opening day of his spectacle. The show was a sight to behold. Every tree had changed to shades of deepest gold and robin red, to sun-kissed yellow and pumpkin orange. As I slowly drove along this festive row, leaves danced in the air and brushed against my windshield. It seemed as if I had landed in Oz. I was strongly tempted to get out and clap at God's imagination.

In *Imagination: Embracing a Theology of Wonder*, Cheryl Forbes encourages us to take a look at the colors around us. God took plain lines, she says, and then "God added light and color, which is another kind of light. There are just a few basic colors from which the almost limitless array of tints and shades come. But don't dismiss light because it provides the shadows, the variations within a color, the depth of certain objects that might otherwise appear flat and uninteresting. Without light, shapes and colors would be meaningless."

A friend tells me of a conversation she had with a woman who had been blind since birth. When the blind woman referred to color, my friend asked her if she understood it; what did she perceive color to be? The sightless woman started describing a color wheel, red being across from green, yellow being across from violet. It seemed she didn't understand it at all! She knew the theory but had no way of seeing the bright delight.

Notice the colors in your world! In *A Natural History of the Senses*, Diane Ackerman tells of visiting a natural history museum: "I once stood in front of a huge piece of sulfur so yellow I began to cry. I wasn't in the least bit unhappy. Quite the opposite; I felt a rush of pleasure and excitement. The intensity of the color affected my nervous system. At the time, I called the emotion wonder, and thought: Isn't it extraordinary to be alive on a planet where there are yellows such as this?" Diane goes on to say that scientists have known for years that certain colors trigger an emotional response. Pink will pacify children. Red excites. Green is calming and restful.

Look around your own home with a new awareness of visual pleasure. What is your favorite color? How can you add a touch of beauty? Poet John Keats said, "A thing of beauty is a joy forever." Miriam Rockness, in *Home: God's Design*, notes, "Touched even fleetingly by 'a thing of beauty' one can be lifted above common routines and petty afflictions. One's spirits can be sustained long after the transcendent moment. We have the power to affect our surroundings; but our surroundings also have the power to affect us."

Yes! Our surroundings affect us, but every one of us can do one small thing to add beauty to our workplace or kitchen or bedroom. File the papers cluttering the desk. Re-cover a pillow. Rearrange the furniture. Light a candle on the dinner table. Or think about your own body. Maybe it's time for a new hairstyle or makeover. It's fun every now and again to find a new look. The makeup counters at the mall will give you a complimentary makeover with no obligation to buy. A friend tells me there's nothing like a professional shoeshine for lifting up a bad day. Open your eyes. Brighten your world.

JOY IN THE TASTE

He . . . fills the hungry with good things.

Psalm 107:9

The apostle Paul writes, "Everything God created is good, and nothing is to be rejected if it is received with thanksgiving, because it is consecrated by the word of God and prayer" (1 Timothy 4:4–5). He's talking about food!

With effusive detail Terry Willits describes a trip to the local farmer's market and then sums up the experience: "It's a Disneyland for the taste buds!"

Whole books are written about the tightrope many of us walk when it comes to food. Of course we must eat to survive. And God has graced us with the ability to enjoy the wide variety of sweets and sours, bitters and blands. Willits continues, "We each have approximately ten thousand tiny taste buds with which to take in the flavors of foods God created." But some of us find so much pleasure in food that we fall prey to the sin of gluttony—much to the delight of diet companies. In *Wishful Thinking*, a fun book of theological definitions, Frederick Buechner says a *glutton* is "one who raids the icebox for a cure for spiritual malnutrition." And in *Disordered Loves*, William S. Stafford says, "Gluttony is eating and drinking that excludes God." He sees trouble when food and drink become "the main means of pleasure in life, the chief source of comfort."

When Jesus himself was famished in the wilderness, the devil asked him to turn stones to bread. Jesus responded with Scripture: "Man does not live on bread alone" (Luke 4:4). Food cannot satisfy the ultimate inner hunger, and yet . . . the gospel stories of Jesus are full of eating, even feasting. He left us with a command to eat and drink bread and wine that represent his body and blood. And we live in hope of joining him at the heavenly marriage supper.

We are encouraged to enjoy the harvest and receive it *with thanksgiving* (1 Timothy 4:4).

Yes, enjoy it. You've got to eat. You've been given the ability to taste—so slow down and let yourself taste the flavors, one bite at a time. Slowly chew and then swallow your food before you put more food on your fork. Don't make a practice of eating on the run or standing at the kitchen sink. Sit down to eat at the table (not in front of the blaring television). At home or in a restaurant try a new dish—a new ingredient or a new combination of old ingredients—just to see if you like it. Go into an ethnic part of town and buy food the names of which you can't even pronounce. Ask questions and experiment. I love Indian food, and Thai food is wonderful. Live a little!

But also enjoy the old standards. Ask your mother, grandmother, or aunts to write down (in their own handwriting) recipes for the dishes you remember from childhood—the family favorites. Pass on to your children your own "food memories." With your children talk about tastes and names of foods and herbs. Welcome them into your kitchen—to share the delight of adding a "pinch" of delight. Grow herbs in a window box and use them as you prepare the family meal.

JOY IN THE SCENTS

Perfume and incense bring joy to the heart.

Proverbs 27:9

Of course taste is so closely connected to smell that sometimes it's hard to distinguish one from another. In her book *Dakota*, Kathleen Norris tells of asking a school class to "make silence"—to think and reflect. The teacher later said her thoughts turned to her mother and "the smells, how this time of year the lingering scent of pickling spices in the house would gradually give way to cinnamon, peppermint, cloves, the smells of Christmas baking. 'It was the candy I loved most . . . nut fudge, caramels, divinity.'" In memory the tastes and smells seemed almost indistinguishable.

Try to identify some of the pleasant scents of your childhood. What can you do to bring those smells into your life now? Plant a lilac bush in your yard? Grow thyme or mint in your garden? Spend an evening cooking? Buy a bit of scented oil or potpourri—a certain brand of soap? Buy a real Christmas tree?

And leave your guests—and children—with the memory imprinted by fragrance. In *Creating a SenseSational Home*, Terry Willits notes: "Twenty years from now others may not remember the fabric that covered your sofa. They most likely won't recall the food you cooked for dinner last week. But if you fill your home with a bounty of fragrance, I assure you they will carry those memories with them long after the scent is gone."

When I think of the gospel story, I see that it's framed in perfume—from the frankincense and myrrh presented by the wise men to the women carrying burial spices and surprised to see an empty tomb.

In her book *Celebrate Joy!* Velma Daniels tells of being drawn by two young children into a bedtime game they called

"God is . . ." They took turns finishing the sentence with positive descriptions of God. Six-year-old Missy finally ventured: "God smells good all the time."

"That's dumb," her older brother said.

But Missy insisted. "Sometimes he smells like orange blossoms and sometimes like apples. Tonight he smells like strawberries."

Velma wonders if Missy was really just enjoying the smell of the strawberry bubble bath that was hardly dry on her skin. But maybe Missy can lead us to a new appreciation of a spiritual metaphor. In 2 Corinthians 2:14–15, Paul writes about godly aroma; God "through us spreads everywhere the fragrance of the knowledge of [Christ]." And then amazingly Paul also says that we believers are "the aroma of Christ."

There's a wonderful gospel story of a woman who poured a pint of expensive perfume on Jesus' feet and then wiped his feet dry with her hair. Was Jesus upset at such a waste? No. Judas Iscariot criticized her—but Jesus came to her defense: "Leave her alone" (John 12:7). All four gospels tell some version of a woman anointing Jesus. The Matthew account ends with Jesus' tribute to her: "Wherever this gospel is preached throughout the world, what she has done will also be told, in memory of her" (Matthew 26:13). Her lavish, fragrant witness is still wafting through the air.

God wants to use you to spread the aroma of Christ. Are you able to joy in that metaphor? In a spiritual sense are you able to exhale as if your breath were springtime fresh?

Can you inhale a little deeper and longer—to enjoy the fragrance yourself?

Velma Daniels relates another conversation with a child. At a Sunday school picnic a young girl gave Velma a bouquet of handpicked wild flowers. Velma gave a big thank you and then suggested the girl go and wash her dirty hands. "I don't want to wash my hands," the girl answered, "because I picked the flowers for you myself, and my hands will smell good all afternoon."

Velma summarizes the lesson she learned that day: "The true reward for a kindness lies not in the thanks you get, but in the memory it leaves on your hands."

Stop the rat race. Enjoy the rich aromas in your life—the ones God gives in nature and the ones God gives through the witness of human kindness.

Stop and enjoy the sights, tastes, and smells of God's good gifts.

GETTING TO JOY

1. Give someone you love a "joy shock." Here's what I mean. In her book *Letters Dropt from God*, Ruth Vaughn tells of her parents living in a nursing home out of state from where Ruth lived. She knew her father loved home-fried fruit pies, and she arranged to hire a woman near the nursing home occasionally to bake and deliver such delicacies to her parents. Ruth says, "This arrangement was a 'constant' until the death of my parents. They never knew when the 'joy shock,' as Mother called such things, would occur." Surprise someone with a treat of the senses—a favorite taste or fragrance or sight.

2. For half an hour today and tomorrow, look at your world as if you were a visitor from another planet. See the natural world, the manmade world, and the beauty in your own home as if you were seeing it for the first time. Talk about "what you see" with a friend or family member. If you can, use a metaphor. (The short-story writer O. Henry said something was "blacker than a raven in a coal mine." Get the picture?)

3. *Creative Teaching Methods* by Marlene LeFever includes a chapter titled "What Colors Are in God?" At the beginning of the chapter Marlene quotes her artist husband as saying, "I hate Bible studies." He continued, "I could tell you what colors are in God, but no one ever asks questions like that." Marlene suggests reading a Bible verse or passage and

asking what colors the passage makes you "see." Try it. What colors does this chapter make you "see"?

4. For a week be very intentional and creative in your meal-time and bedtime thanksgiving. You might draw on the "thanks" of other people by dipping into a book of written prayers.

5. For your family—or for dinner guests—cook and festively present a meal that brings you fond memories of taste and smell. Talk about the food, what it reminds you of, why it is important to you, what special ingredients it takes, how you simmered it all day.... Share your delight. Or invite three close friends to dinner. Ask one to bring an appetizer, one a soup or salad, one a main course, and you provide dessert. Ask each one to bring a dish that has a special memory and to share that as you eat together.

CHAPTER 14

JOY IN RETREAT

*I say to myself, "The L*ORD *is my portion; therefore I will wait
for him." The L*ORD *is good to those whose hope is in him, to
the one who seeks him.*

Lamentations 3:24–25

The mightiest works of God are the fruit of silence.

F. B. Meyer

꒜

Come on, jump. I'll be there!" Bobbie called to me. I stood
on the edge of the swimming pool, heart pounding in my
ears. I looked at the water. I looked in Bobbie's eyes. He was
willing me to trust him, to let go and dive into the chlorinated
water that made my eyes sting even from a distance. I wanted
to do it, but I was too afraid. This experience as a sixteen-year-
old girl whose school friend was trying to teach her to dive was
a mini parable to me of my future relationship with Christ.
"Come on, Sheila, jump. I'll be there."

"But where is *there?*" I ask. "And will I like it when I get
there?" Loss of control. It terrifies us. But to truly enter into
retreat with Christ demands that we surrender control and be
with God whatever that will look like.

In *Prayer and the Pursuit of Happiness*, Richard Harries says,
"Most of us find it difficult to use silence well. Our minds wan-
der all over the place and unless we are careful we simply create a vacuum in the mind in which all kinds of unwanted fears

and spites come in. Yet it is above all in silence that life can begin to take on depth."

I look back on my own life and remember how scary it used to be to be quiet. As long as I stayed busy and noisy, I didn't have to face things that were painful to think about. Because I couldn't see an answer, I just kept going, kept my mind full of stuff. That's control. It's saying to God, "I can't see an answer to this, but I'm not going to stop and fall at your feet and admit that my life is out of control. That would be too frightening, so I'll just keep going." When I finally lost control and fell at Jesus' feet, I found out that it was painful but also a huge relief. I exchanged my manic repetition of "I can do this, I can do this!" to "I can't do this, I can't do this!" and found out that Jesus can and will if we will move aside. From that place alone we can move into quiet retreat with Christ.

To find the joy that comes with quiet retreat in the presence of God—we have to be willing to stop. We have to be willing to listen.

I talked to a friend about this recently. We were driving to another friend's house, and I took the opportunity to voice a concern. "Do you see how busy your life has become?" I asked her. "You never stop and take a day off or even a few hours to read a book or watch the fall leaves change color."

"I can't be quiet," she said. "It's too stressful."

"What do you mean?" I pursued. "How is quiet stressful?" I could tell she was uncomfortable with our discussion.

"I'd just rather keep busy," she said.

Quiet is like an item that hasn't sold well and sits at the back of the shelf, dusty and out-of-date.

Miriam Rockness *(Keep These Things, Ponder Them in Your Heart)* expresses the exhaustion of many women I meet. In identifying her problem, Miriam also reaches toward her solution:

> I am depleted.... The well has run dry!...
>
> I know what has gone wrong. I have continued to give out without renewing my inner resources. Can one breathe out without breathing in? I need to draw apart

from everyone, everything, and nourish my soul. I've told myself solitude is a luxury I can't afford. But my poverty of spirit declares solitude as necessary for my soul as food is for the body. Solitude. A time to remove myself from distraction. To order my day. My week. My life. To get in touch with myself. With my Maker.

In this world of clamor how do we find quiet places alone with God? A quiet place—away from the noise of the world. In his *Screwtape Letters*, C. S. Lewis imagines that the devils plot to banish music and silence and replace them with noise. "We [the devils] will make the whole universe noise in the end." Noise can distract us, crowd us, irritate us—jangle our nerves.

It's time all of us learned a bit more about how to retreat—and be alone with God. What is retreat? It's taking time away from our normal routine. It's making a date with God that nothing will be allowed to intrude on. It can be as simple as setting aside an afternoon to go to the park with a journal, your Bible, a favorite devotional book. Or just sitting under a tree and enjoying the presence of God. It can be walking along a beach conscious of the companionship of Christ.

Some of my friends have had the opportunity to go on retreat with a spiritual director with whom you talk for an hour a day. Otherwise, it's you and God. No dinner chat. No breakfast banter. It can be hard to know how to be quiet, where to begin. I think it's like mountain climbing. You start slowly, and it might be helpful to have a guide who's been up these slopes before; that's why the trained spiritual director is there and available.

My friend Brennan Manning leads directed silent retreats. A group of five or six spends a few days in quiet prayer and meditation, reading Scripture and portions of books he sets out. Then each day he meets with each retreatant privately to talk over whatever the Holy Spirit brings to mind, or to offer help in learning how to be quiet.

I asked one of my friends to give me some feedback after his first retreat with Brennan. "Pain and joy," he said. "Pain and joy."

"I'll need more than that!" I laughed.

"All right, let me try and put it into words." He was quiet for a few moments. "I've been a Christian for a long time, as you know. This is the first time I felt I really met with God. I was embarrassed at first. Left alone with God hour after hour, it was embarrassing to realize how little I knew him or had let him know me. I didn't know what to say. I prayed for everyone I could think of and then I ran out. Brennan encouraged me to just 'be' with God." He stopped for a moment and looked at me, I imagine to see if I understood what he was saying.

"The first two days were difficult and long, but then I could relax and enjoy the presence of God. The pain was facing my own humanity and sin, but the joy was in beginning to accept the love and grace of God. I had no idea," he said, his eyes shining, "no idea I was so loved!"

I hope to be able to be part of a group like this soon. I travel so much and, with a baby boy, a whole day of retreat is rare, but I know that joy waits for us in quiet places.

Perhaps like me you can't immediately carve out two or five days, but we can all carve out an afternoon or an evening and purpose to be with God so that he can remind us just how much he is with us.

Try to allow some of your quiet time to be out of doors—seeing God at work in and through his creation. Allow God to speak to you through his handiwork. Romans 1:20 says, "For since the creation of the world God's invisible qualities—his eternal power and divine nature—have been clearly seen, being understood from what has been made."

I think of this message Anne Morrow Lindbergh sensed from a sea shell, as recorded in her book *Gift from the Sea:* "You will remind me that I must try to be alone for part of each year, even a week or a few days; and for part of each day, even for an hour or a few minutes in order to keep my core, my center, my island-quality. You will remind me that unless I keep the island-quality somewhere within me, I will have little to give my husband, my children, my friends or the world at large."

In a book of essays, *The God of Stones and Spiders*, Chuck Colson tells the story of Nien Cheng, a Chinese woman thrown in a small dank prison cell in 1966 during the Cultural Revolution. (Not the kind of solitude I'm wishing for you.) Her attention turned to a pea-sized spider spinning an intricate web. "I had just watched an architectural feat by an extremely skilled artist." That spider turned her thoughts off herself and to God the Creator. "I knew I had just witnessed something that was extraordinarily beautiful and uplifting. I thanked God for what I had just seen. It helped me to see that He was in control. Mao Zedong and his revolutionaries seemed much less menacing. I felt a renewal of hope and confidence."

Colson continues, saying Nien's story is about her own faith and courage—but more, it's a story about "God who can speak even through a spider's handiwork."

I encourage you to let God speak to you in the quiet—as you read his Word, as you glean the wisdom of other saints, as you listen to the Spirit within your heart, as you observe the handiwork of God's creation.

Give yourself a retreat.

"Be still, and know that I am God" (Psalm 46:10).

Joy in the quiet away from the noise
of the phone and the traffic
the screams of small boys.
Joy in his presence
alone, face to face,
renewed in the quiet
and reborn in grace.

GETTING TO JOY

1. Find two or three friends who would like to share a retreat and plan on a weekend away. It could be at a hotel or a borrowed home of a friend, just somewhere away from the norm. Choose a favorite spiritual classic or devotional book and agree to read a certain passage each day. Spend time

alone with God reading and praying. In the evening come together and share your thoughts and needs and pray for each other.

2. Keep a joy journal. As you learn to spend time alone with God, write down the things that the Holy Spirit brings to mind that bring you joy. Share those with others around you. Write letters to friends reminding them of all that we have to be joyful about.

3. Choose a particular television program that you enjoy and give that time to God. Turn the TV off and be quiet with him. At the beginning and the end of that time, sing a hymn that you love to the Lord.

4. Mark your calendar and set aside a specific time to be with God. For me one of those times is New Year's Eve. I spend a couple of hours alone with the Lord looking back over the year. I thank him for his grace and mercy and commit the new year to him.

5. In *Prayer and the Pursuit of Happiness*, Richard Harries suggests a ten-second retreat, based on the Scripture of Mark 4. "Those who like to use their imagination in prayer (which is not everyone) can picture themselves in a boat, with the anxieties which are beating upon their mind as waves. Then Christ stands in our soul and says, 'Peace, be still.' This method should not be dismissed as a technique, or derided as a piece of self-indoctrination. It is simply a way of apprehending, through the imagination, a spiritual truth." He continues, "The purpose of silence is to lead us into stillness and the purpose of stillness is to help us become more aware of God." Try it.

CHAPTER 15
JOY IN FRIENDSHIP

How can we thank God enough for you in return for all the
joy we have in the presence of our God because of you?
1 Thessalonians 3:9

✢

In her wonderful classic *The Christian's Secret of a Happy Life*, Hannah Whitall Smith noted that human beings around us are often the bottles that hold the medicine God has prescribed for us. I agree!

In a letter to his friend Arthur Greeves, C. S. Lewis said, "Friendship to me is the chief happiness of life.... If I had to give a piece of advice to a young man about a place to live, I think I should say sacrifice almost everything to live where you can be near your friends."

Barry and I moved to Tennessee for two reasons. To be closer to his mom and dad, as it's important to us that they be part of the earliest painting of Christian's life. And to be near friends. Most of my best friends live in or near Nashville—and these friends make my life very rich indeed. There is nothing in this world I enjoy more than being with those I love and who love me. The apostle John knew the pain of being distant from his friends and the joy of "getting together." The short letter of 2 John ends: "I hope to visit you and talk with you face to face, so that our joy may be complete." And the apostle Paul longed to see his friends in Philippi; he addresses them as "you whom I love and long for, my joy and crown" (Philippians 4:1).

On the radio Chuck Swindoll used the phrase "a sheltering tree" to describe a need we all have. I love the picture that it paints of friendship. What a joy for two people—each to be a shady covering for the other. A place to rest when the sun is too hot or the wind too biting.

But the "friendship factor" apparently enhances more than joie de vivre. The September-October 1997 issue of *Modern Maturity* (no, I do not regularly read this magazine) quotes researchers and professors at length, saying that friendship is good for your health—even your cardiovascular and immune systems. "The evidence is clear: Good friends are critically important to successful aging," concludes writer R. Daniel Foster.

We need good friends even if we have wonderful husbands. It's a mistake for husbands or wives to walk away from all other relationships in the belief that now they have a full-time friend! We need the companionship of others in the body of Christ. We need other women to laugh and cry with.

Of course friendship is not always comfortable—as we speak the truth to each other—but when we're all anchored in the same harbor, we're able to help each other patch the holes in our boats. If a friend has hurt my feelings, I find it hard to be honest about that. I'd rather just push it under the carpet and move on. Sometimes that's appropriate; there's no need to make a soap opera out of every moment. But sometimes speaking the truth about a hurt is very important. It's risky stuff. *What if my friend walks away? What if I'm wrong? What if she gets angry?* None of these human thoughts should keep us from our commitment to really love in all its colors. When we can walk through that field with a few thorns in the grass and make it to the other side, our friendships will be stronger and our joy will be real.

I love the friendship that is springing up among the six of us who make up the team of Women of Faith. Some, like Luci Swindoll and Marilyn Meberg, have been friends for years. When I showed up in Hawaii with a stroller, a car seat, and a bag of diapers, I was the newcomer, and they welcomed me in.

Most of the time we laugh and gather the jewels of wisdom and wit that each one brings, but we've also had difficult moments that we've had to thrash out together. The key to me is the security of the bond. We are here for the long haul.

Some nights I'll be sitting at my desk. It's late and I'm tired. The phone will ring and it will be Patsy Clairmont with a joke or something inspiring she read in a book that she wants to share with me. She puts wind back into my sails. If I'm struggling with an attitude or confused about how to handle tension in a relationship, I'll pick up the phone and call Marilyn Meberg. It's great to have a shrink for a friend!

Luci Swindoll wasn't able to be with us on two of the Joyful Journey weekends in '97 and we missed her so much. The first time she missed we were sitting in the backstage area, waiting for the program to begin, feeling sorry for ourselves because our buddy was missing—and right then she called one of our cell phones. We were like a bunch of kids rushing each other to "get off" so we could have our turn to say, "Hi, we miss you. We love you. Don't do this again!" I have all of their photographs on my refrigerator door. Every time I reach in for the milk for my tea or Christian's bottle, they smile at me. Having them in my life makes me feel connected, loved, understood, covered, accepted, anchored. Friends are life and joy to our souls.

One of the deepest callings of friendship is to weep with those who weep. As I write, in autumn, I watch the leaves falling off my favorite tree outside my window. And so there are seasons in all of our lives when the wind blows cold and we feel fragile and exposed. These are the times when we wrap each other up in a blanket of love and friendship and stay right there until the buds begin to show again.

Real friendship grows when we are prepared to be there equally in the bad moments and the good, when we weep with those who weep—and rejoice with those who rejoice (see Romans 12:15).

Sometimes it's difficult to rejoice with someone else. But when we are secure in Christ, we can celebrate when someone else does well, even if it's something we wished for ourselves. That is a sacrifice, a gift of love.

I remember when I was nominated for a Grammy Award in the same category as my friend Sandi Patty. I was so excited, bought a beautiful dress, made sure all my family in Scotland was watching, wrote my little speech thanking everyone from my first Sunday school teacher to the entire Billy Graham organization. The night itself was something special. I was four rows behind Barbra Streisand, and every time she turned and exposed that famous profile I wanted to burst into "People, people who need people."

Then it was time for the announcement in our category. A camera man positioned himself at my side to capture my surprised look. "And the winner is ... Sandi Patty." I clapped ferociously, even as all sorts of thoughts went through my head ... *I wish I hadn't spent so much on this dumb dress. I hope my mom's not too disappointed. Barbra's not going to see me now.* But, honestly, after the words sank in, as I watched Sandi up there telling her kids via television to go to bed now, I was really happy for her and I knew she deserved it.

When the event was over that night, those nominated were invited to a fancy party at a restaurant called Spago's in Beverly Hills. It was a real who's who. Janet Jackson was at the table next to mine, as was the British pop star Sting. Everyone floated from table to table kissing and hugging; it was hilarious. Those who won were getting drunk to celebrate and those who lost were getting drunk to mollify themselves. I was definitely out of place with my Diet Coke, and I left before it got too hairy.

I didn't see Sandi that night. She went to a different party. As I drove home with my feet aching from being in pointy-toed high heels, I ran the whole day over again in my mind. *It would be fun to win a Grammy*, I thought. *But Sandi honestly deserved it. Knowing me, I would have tripped going up the stairs and looked like a goofball. I can't wait to get home and have a nice cup of tea and a hot bath.* I made a mental note to call and congratulate Sandi. I called in a couple of days and told her that I was happy for her. She was her usual gracious self and told me she liked my dress!

When we're secure in God's love, we can cheer for each other, knowing that our Father's eyes are on us too.

Ann Hibbard notes, "I know of no better way to deepen a friendship than to regularly join with a friend in prayer." In her book *Treasured Friends*, she quotes Juanita, a lonely homemaker. Not long after Juanita prayed, asking God for a friend, an acquaintance with whom she had little in common (a divorced woman with no children) asked Juanita if she would be her prayer partner. "We've met every week for an hour for the past five years. We talk about our lives and our needs or joys, and we pray for each other. It has to be early in the morning, but neither of us would miss it for the world.

"I've seen my friend grow in confidence and healing of her pain. . . . And God's taken my loneliness away. It's been a gift from my loving Lord."

If you sense there's something in your spirit blocking you from receiving the joy of the Lord—from knowing the reality of his love—ask good, godly friends for a specific prayer of blessing. A woman recently told me of a major spiritual breakthrough that came as she humbled herself enough to ask two friends to place their hands on her and claim God's blessing on her and for her. "Something happened," she says. No immediate emotional or spiritual change, but since then she has had a new awareness of his presence and a heaviness of spirit has lifted. As James 5:16 says, "Confess your sins to each other and pray for each other so that you may be healed. The prayer of a righteous man is powerful and effective."

Allow God to work through your friends—always listening for the discernment of the Spirit within and to his guidance in the Word.

All intimate relationships leave us vulnerable to some extent. The ache that we have to be known will never be fully satisfied by our human relationships, and accepting that has been a key to joy for me. We were formed for relationship, but it's unreasonable to imagine that any one man or woman can be everything to us. We were formed for relationship but *we are filled in Christ*. Our deepest needs for intimacy will be met only in the "friend who sticks closer than a brother" (Proverbs 18:24). The One who has surely carried our sorrows. The One who has known us since before we were born.

GETTING TO JOY

1. Henry Ward Beecher said: "Do not keep the alabaster boxes of your love and tenderness sealed up until your friends are dead. Fill their lives with sweetness. Speak approving cheering words while their ears can hear them and while their hearts can be thrilled with them." Every day this week call one friend—or potential friend—and express "approving cheering words" that lift her spirits and yours.

2. If you don't have friends, reach out and be a friend. Do a kind deed simply for the sake of sharing the love of Christ—not with expectations that you are "buying" a friend. Give a smile. Just "be there" for someone. Albert Schweitzer said, "[One] must not try to force his way into the personality of another. . . . The soul, too, has its clothing of which we must not deprive it."

3. Ask someone to be a partner in prayer. For starters, "partner" for a specific length of time—maybe three months. The relationship may or may not become a deep friendship. If it does, consider yourself blessed.

4. Organize an informal get-together of your childhood, high school, or college friends. Or at least find them and write them a letter. Reconnect by reminiscing and laughing. And establish things you have in common still today.

5. Bring a group of women to a Women of Faith conference and share it together. One reason we speakers love it is because we get to be with each other and enter into each other's stories. Take an evening after the weekend and debrief together: What gifts did you receive from the weekend and from each other?

CHAPTER 16

JOY IN CELEBRATING MILESTONES

Samuel took a stone and set it up between Mizpah and Shen. He
named it Ebenezer, saying, "Thus far has the LORD helped us."
1 Samuel 7:12

In our church back home we sometimes sang an old hymn
called "Come Thou Fount of Every Blessing." It has some
wonderful lines—but then there's one that made us teenagers
roll our eyes because it sounded so weird, "Here I raise my
Ebenezer; Hither by thy help I'm come." Whatever it meant,
it was old-fashioned, left over from another century, and
couldn't have any relevance to here and now.

But it does! After the Lord had defeated the Philistines by
frightening them and routing them with a great "thunder,"
Samuel raised an Ebenezer. What does it mean? He set up a
"stone of help"—a marker that celebrated a breakthrough and
thanked God for a victory. For years to come that stone was
a reminder of God's faithfulness to his people.

STONES OF REMEMBRANCE

I've heard of congregations that have reclaimed the idea
of raising Ebenezers—putting piles of stones in the yard of the
church to commemorate significant events. One church did
this so often it started to have a hard time mowing the lawn!

My in-laws "can't throw anything out," because everything has sentimental value to them, from Barry's school books, to ancient Christmas ornaments that look as if they decorated the ark. There may be such a thing as going overboard, but I for one find value in keeping a few select mementos that remind me of where I've been and how God has been with me.

What mementos do you keep in a box in the closet that you might bring out and showcase in your home? If you're one of those people who "keeps everything," rotate some of your favorites in and out of boxes—so you can enjoy one or two at a time, savoring the unique quality of each memory.

I'm a lover of books, but I have a few special ones set out on display because of the role they've played in my life. Books like *Hinds' Feet on High Places* by Hannah Hurnard, which reminds me of my time in college. God used this book to encourage me as an idealistic young Christian who wanted to change the world overnight. Through the experience of the character named Much-Afraid, I began to understand that life is a journey, not a puzzle that can be worked out by bedtime.

I have photos in frames all over the house, but a couple are placed strategically because of what they say to me. My grandmother's photo is by my bed, and when I'm feeling tired or discouraged, I'll look at her and smile and remember the long line of godly women I am privileged to come from. I have a collection of small silver boxes handmade in Wales. I keep them out even though they are a pain to dust, because they were all given to me by my mom and my sister, Frances, and as I dust them I pray for both of them.

Sometimes we keep those "special" things tucked away to protect them, but it's good for us to be surrounded by memories of God's faithfulness and the love of others.

MOMENTS TO REMEMBER

These mementos remind me of God's faithfulness in the past, but as I get older—and now that I have a child—I'm also increasingly aware of the importance of consciously celebrating events and anniversaries, making the celebrations themselves *moments* of joy here and now. (The physical mementos and the fond memories will just be the extra bonus.)

In *Why Not Celebrate?* Sara Wenger Shenk asks some more basic questions.

> How do we celebrate peoplehood? How do we celebrate God's good earth? How do our children develop a sense of identity that runs deeper than the latest fad? How can we give them a heritage with firmer roots than the current peer group?
>
> These are questions that go to the heart of what celebration is about. Celebration is the honoring of that which we hold most dear. Celebration is delighting in that which tells us who we are. Celebration is taking the time to cherish each other. Celebration is returning with open arms and thankful hearts to our Maker.

I turned forty in the summer of '96. Contrary to the popular dread of this milestone, I looked forward to it. I was enjoying this season of life. I was comfortable in my own slippers. I had planned to spend the day with my friends Marlene and Carolyn, having afternoon tea and doing "girl" things. In the evening we would be joined by Barry and Marlene's husband, Frank, for dinner at my favorite Italian restaurant. I had no idea that Barry had worked hard for weeks planning a surprise party. I've not had a party since I was a child, and it never crossed my mind to suspect a thing.

We "girls" had a fun day. We went to a very fancy hotel by the ocean and drank tea and ate strawberry tarts, then went off to the spa to take my forty-year-old frame in for its 40,000 mile service. I was eager to get home and change for dinner and couldn't understand why Marlene was driving so slowly. We could have been overtaken by dogs!

Eventually we made it home, and we decided to go into the house through the garage instead of the front door. Marlene was carrying a package so she kicked the door with her foot hoping Barry would hear her. He opened the door, let out a yell, and slammed it in her face! I thought he'd finally lost his marbles. I used my key and let us in. I was about to tell Barry that he owed Marlene a nose job when I walked into the company of forty of my friends who burst into "Happy birthday to you." It was a great evening. When it was all over and the last piece of cake had been scraped off the carpet, I lay in a bubble bath, letting the day wash over me. So many faces, so many memories, so many years of friendship. There were friends there from Open Doors, a ministry to the church in lands where Christians are persecuted for their faith. There were friends from the board I served on which reaches out to those who are HIV positive. There were friends from seminary. There were greeting faxes from friends who couldn't be there . . . Bill and Gloria Gaither, Ruth Graham. Friends at CBN sent a video of five years of hairstyles on *The 700 Club*, a scary sight!

As I lay with bubbles up to my ears, I felt so rich. Every face reminded me of God's goodness to me. Some of us had been through tough times together, but we were still friends. I was grateful to Barry for making me take a pause in my life to celebrate the day in a way I will never forget.

In *The Return of the Prodigal Son*, Henri Nouwen says, "Celebration belongs to God's Kingdom. God not only offers forgiveness, reconciliation, and healing, but wants to lift up these gifts as a source of joy for all who witness them." I love what George MacDonald said: "It is the heart that is not yet sure of its God that is afraid to laugh in His presence."

We Christians might look a bit more redeemed if we learned more about partying well—finding ways to celebrate the victories and milestones in each other's lives and also celebrating the traditional (and maybe some untraditional) seasonal holidays and holy days.

Families can celebrate their own events: anniversaries, Mother's Day, Father's Day. My mom has a collection of odd little items that Frances, Stephen, and I bought or made for her at school for Mother's Day when we were children. As the years passed we were able to afford nicer gifts, but I know that those misshapen pieces of pottery have a special place in her heart—reminders of the particular moments when we celebrated her very being in our lives.

I'm grateful for the advent of video cameras. We have a visual diary of the first year of Christian's life from his birth to his first jar of carrots, his first crawl, his first tooth, his first hair trim. I wonder though why we save those camcorders just for babies? Wouldn't it be fun to capture moments with all our family, with friends? I'm taking as much footage as I can for Christian of his two grandmas and his grandpa. Photos are great, but when he's older and they're perhaps no longer with us I want him to be able to remember them as they really were. I want him to hear their voices and see that twinkle in their eyes when they talk to him.

Why don't you make yourself the cinematographer for your family? It would be fun if someone has a special birthday coming up to tape a short message from all his or her loved ones, even those seen every day, and make that film your gift. Suggest the gift receiver pull it out on those "nothing in my life is working" days and be bathed in the love and comfort of friends.

Our celebrations can and should also reach out beyond our families to our community of friends and acquaintances. In Luke 15 three parallel parables end in great rejoicing—not just a solitary person or family knowing the joy of the Lord—but a community affair. "Rejoice with me," says the shepherd to his friends and neighbors, "I have found my lost sheep." "Rejoice with me," says a woman who has swept her house top to bottom, "I have found my lost coin." "Let's have a feast and celebrate," says a wealthy father, "for this son of mine was dead and is alive again."

Celebrate! I know, putting on a party, even an informal gathering, takes effort, from organizing to cleanup. But I think our society, even our church, is hungry for meaningful interaction. Forget the virtual internet party. Have a real one that includes smiles, laughter, and popcorn. Let people gather around the grill. Skewer their own shish kebabs. Make their own pizzas. Decorate their own Christmas cookies. Or decorate your Christmas tree with you.

One of my favorite Christmas memories is the year that my friends Amy and Andrew Gaither Hayes invited me to their tree-trimming night. We laughed as we pulled out old ornaments, and they told the stories behind them. I laughed as they argued over where to put the lights of the tree. Andrew had brought his lights into their marriage—big, manly lights—and Amy loved the small pretty lights and kept moving Andrew's to the back of the tree. Then we sat together as Amy read *A Child's Christmas in Wales* by Dylan Thomas. They gave me a great gift that year by inviting me into their celebration. It was the year before I met Barry, and I was living alone. Why not share the goodness of God in your life with others? It takes no money to string popcorn, but the gift is the fellowship.

In a novel about African tribal life, *Things Fall Apart*, Chinua Achebe gives an interesting perspective on parties: Someone who brings people together for a feast "does not do so to save them from starving. They all have food in their own homes. When we gather together in the moonlit village ground it is not because of the moon. Every man can see it in his own compound. We come together because it is good for kinsmen to do so."

We gather to celebrate because we are made for community.

Sign on, sign up for the party. Celebrate the moment. Set up a milestone. Treasure the memory. Share the joy.

GETTING TO JOY

1. To commemorate someone's birthday, write an acrostic, using the letters of the person's name to represent positive qualities you appreciate in him or her. Include the acrostic in your card—or weave it into the message of a handmade card. To get you started, remember that

Jesus
Others
You

is an acrostic of the word *joy*. And here's my personal best:

Brave
Astute
Risk-taker
Really silly
Yummy!!!

2. In *Turn Off the TV*, Kathy Bence suggests celebrating with children the first and last days of the school year. "Hold an annual family picnic the first evening of school. Be sure to have the same menu and use the same location. Encourage children to set goals for the school year and promise (nonmaterial) rewards for the accomplishment of those goals." And "take the children out to lunch the last day of school." Let them choose the place—preferably the same place every year.

3. By yourself or with your family or friends do something to make Sunday a weekly celebration of rest. Worship yes, but also set specific "sabbath" rituals. In *Keeping the Sabbath Wholly*, Marva Dawn remembers "Sunday was always special in my childhood simply because of the delight of anticipation in our family's customary Saturday-night tasks—for me, those included taking a special bath, curling my hair, and setting out my best clothes to wear in the morning. I wish every child could grow up with that sense of delight in expectation of holy worship. The very habits of my home imbued me with a sense of the holy."

4. Marva Dawn notes: "Festival involves the paradoxical combination of tradition and creativity." Take an established tradition of yours and give an ever-so-slightly new twist. Buy a new ribbon for an old wreath. Add a relish to your Thanksgiving dinner. Each year ask a different family member to

make place cards for Thanksgiving or Christmas dinner. Then save the cards as mementos. Ask them to be as creative as possible.

5. Next time you find something you had lost, call for a celebration. Have a Lost-and-Found Party, reminiscent of the three parables in Luke 15. Introducing a prayer of "grace," tell your guests why you've called them together. As favors, you could have candy coins—Necco wafers or foil-covered chocolates. Don't take life for granted. Celebrate!

EPILOGUE

Joy to the world! That's what we sing every Christmas. Young boys in choir robes sing it uncomfortably. The message blares through the loud speakers in the mall. The angels sang it, and the demons dread it. Joy. It's a powerful force. It looks in the face of life with all its tears and tragedy, all its ups and downs, and it wraps a blanket of eternal comfort around our shoulders. It doesn't leave the scene. Joy in the midst of pain, in the presence of questions, on the faces of our friends, in the quiet moments of our days. This gift the world seeks after and sells its soul to buy—found in the arms of the One who is joy. Don't look for it apart from God. It cannot breathe without his air. It has no substance without his presence.

I see a figure running round and round a beautiful castle wondering what would be the best way to find access knowing that she has no right to be there. Exhausted from attempting to scale walls and break through windows, she falls at the door.

207

It opens, and she is invited to come in and sit beside the King. He takes his robe off and wraps it around her fragile shoulders, puts a ring on her finger and a crown on her head. No worth and made worthy—at the same moment. This is joy. This is our life.

If you have made your way through this book and you still have no real relationship with the King, the Joy Giver, it's very simple. You can run around the castle a few more times, or you can stop and knock at the door and ask him to let you in. That's what I did. They called it prayer. It was talking. Talking to God. It was admitting that I couldn't make it on my own and I didn't want to. I thanked him for loving me and asked him to teach me how to love him, and it began. What a journey it has been. What a journey it continues to be. For the King's children the best is always yet to be.

The Book of Common Prayer includes a beautiful prayer for evening that requests God's help in various circumstances: "Tend the sick, Lord Christ, give rest to the weary, bless the dying, soothe the suffering, pity the afflicted, shield the joyous; and all for your love's sake. Amen."

Did you hear it? It was in there. It's my prayer for you. I tuck it into this page for you with all the love of heaven: *shield the joyous*. I pray: Wrap them up, dear Lord. Keep them safe and kind and hopeful. Speak to them in the quiet and in the noise and in all the moments of their days ... for your sake. Amen.

So until we meet again—

"To him who is able to keep you from falling and to present you before his glorious presence without fault and *with great joy*—to the only God our Savior be glory, majesty, power and authority, through Jesus Christ our Lord, before all ages, now and forevermore! Amen" (Jude 24–25, emphasis added).